10/02

Richard Yates

Twayne's United States Authors Series

Frank Day, Editor

Clemson University

TUSAS 669

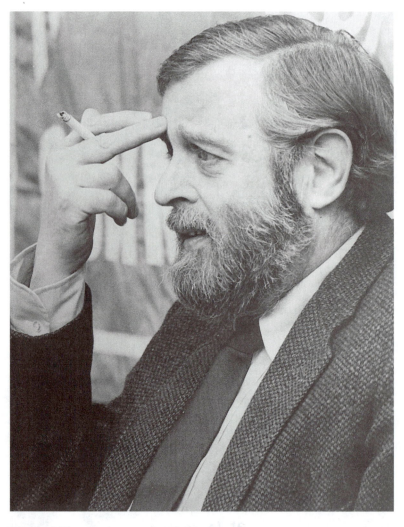

RICHARD YATES
Courtesy of John A. Williams

Chapter 1

Richard Yates, An American Realist (1926–1992)

Richard Yates's nine works of fiction are a comprehensive account of American middle-class character and fate from the Great Depression to the early 1970s. The child of a broken home—and a lifelong observer of dislocations and disorders—he told stories about psychologically and socially stifled people living in an atmosphere of official optimism. His struggling characters are anti-Roosevelt when "happy days are here again," convictionless when America is at war, and most at home with the cool restlessness or inertia of the 1950s; the commitments of the 1960s drive them back into their worlds of private frustration. Without the energy of the New Deal or the New Frontier, they seem marooned in a permanent time of doubt: their defining moments come before hope is kindled or after its flame burns down. Their first appearances, in the novel *Revolutionary Road* and the short story volume *Eleven Kinds of Loneliness,* set the course of Yates's career. Their last depictions, in *Uncertain Times,* Yates's unfinished novel about his experience as Robert F. Kennedy's speechwriter in 1963, confirm a writer's vision of Americans at cross-purposes with each other and with their culture.

The title *Revolutionary Road* seems to portend a bold manifesto, and its main characters, Columbia-educated Frank Wheeler and onetime aspiring acting student April Wheeler, at first blush seem to display originality and vigor.[1] Marrying young, they leave Manhattan for the post–World War II dream of suburban freedom, peace, space, and charm. But Revolutionary Road, a classy and expensive district in Connecticut, turns out to be a cozy nightmare, complete with insipid neighbors and a nearby vulgar housing development.[2] Cut off from the sustaining idealism associated with a revolutionary early America, the Wheelers live instead in a 1950s world of pastel cars and houses, estranged from their vague expectations of a better life. They struggle to be interesting and authentic, but are eventually pulled down by the undertow of their own illusions and the monotony of their white bread community. The high point of their lives comes when they patronize their less sophisticated neighbors and design an elaborate escape route from suburbia to Europe.

Yates's contemporaries tend to ascribe grand designs and mystic visions to their protagonists: Saul Bellow's *Henderson the Rain King* and Norman Mailer's *Why Are We in Vietnam?* exemplify such overreaching. Yates concentrates instead on his characters' fears and frustrations and, ultimately, on the limitations of their imaginations. Frank and April fervently wish to escape to Europe, but their Europe is a shimmering illusion, formed more by the romantic longings of their parents' generation than by any genuine urges of their own. At their most idealistic, Frank and April want merely to conform to some cultural fantasy of rebellion, of originality, of creativity. Their delusions are quickly exposed.

Yates's first two books, *Revolutionary Road* and *Eleven Kinds of Loneliness,* mark off the territory that he explored for a lifetime. His stories of the 1950s, *Eleven Kinds of Loneliness,* published in 1962, study the lopsided lives and thwarted ambitions of other Americans in the middle: a daydreaming cabby, a well-intentioned but complacent young schoolteacher, a neurotic army sergeant, and a variety of trapped office workers. Such characters cherish their private obsessions and compulsions, comfort themselves with meaningless conventions and clichés, immerse themselves in the hum and buzz of empty sociability, and find ways to dodge the futilities of their jobs and marriages. Like the Wheelers, they specialize in denial and endure every variety of disappointment available in their time.

These two books describe America's least conspicuous victims. With highly concentrated purpose, Yates thereafter devoted his entire career to throwing into high relief the hidden injuries of class, including bleak childhoods, nothing jobs, and barren landscapes. Combining the brooding reflections of a Theodore Dreiser with the deft touch of a Gustave Flaubert, he observed struggling Americans as matter-of-factly as Dreiser did in describing Sister Carrie's train ride to Chicago and with the same exquisite craftsmanship as Flaubert showed in describing Emma Bovary's Sunday afternoon in the village of Tostes. Raw naturalism and subtle craftsmanship—seemingly incompatible qualities—join to make Yates one of the most accomplished writers of the post–World War II period.

Yates practiced realism in an age when the mode was retreating before the onslaughts of such postmodern experimental writers as Thomas Pynchon and Donald Barthelme. Of course some vestiges of realism remained. There was New Journalism by Tom Wolfe and Joan Didion,

Richard Yates

David Castronovo and Steven Goldleaf

Pace University

Twayne Publishers
An Imprint of Simon & Schuster Macmillan
New York

Prentice Hall International
London • Mexico City • New Delhi • Singapore • Sydney • Toronto

Twayne's United States Author Series No. 669

Richard Yates
David Castronovo and Steven Goldleaf

Twayne Publishers
An Imprint of Simon & Schuster Macmillan
1633 Broadway
New York, New York 10019

Library of Congress Cataloging-in-Publication Data

Castronovo, David.
    Richard Yates / David Castronovo and Steven Goldleaf.
        p. cm. — (Twayne's United States authors series ; TUSAS 669)
    Includes bibliographical references and index.
    ISBN 0-8057-4031-7
    1. Yates, Richard, 1926– —Criticism and interpretation.
    I. Goldleaf, Steven.   II. Title.   III. Series.
    PS3575.A83Z6 1996
    823'.54—dc20   95-38515
                                                                        CIP

10 9 8 7 6 5 4 3 2 1

Printed in the United States of America

For Elizabeth and Olivia and Genevieve

Contents

Acknowledgments

We have had a good deal of thoughtful assistance in researching Richard Yates: DeWitt Henry, Leslie Epstein, and John A. Williams helped us piece together chronologies and supplied many interesting details; Willie Williams, Susan Monsky, and Patricia Borns helped us trace Yates's trail in Boston, and helped us locate his former students there, doing so cheerfully and with old affection; the staff of Mugar Library's Special Collections Department at Boston University helped us negotiate their archival matter both from Yates and Yates's agent, Monica McCall; the reference staff of Henry Birnbaum Library at Pace University, especially Michelle Fanelli, Elisabeth Birnbaum, Tom Snyder, and Suzanne Marchese, were often ingenious in tracking down obscure bits of data; James Kahn helped in many ways, not least being his suggestion that we read Kunstler's useful book on suburbia; Mitch Douglas of ICM opened his correspondence files and sharp memory to us, and was consistently generous in his suggestions of sources we might contact; Dr. Herman Joseph of the Rockefeller University offered his detailed knowledge of Erving Goffman; and the Dean's Office of Dyson College, Pace University, provided much welcome cooperation and financial assistance.

Chronology

1964–71 Teaches creative writing at the University of Iowa.

1965 Hospitalized from August through October in UCLA's Neuropsychiatric Institute.

1965–66 Writes screenplays for Columbia Pictures.

1966 Receives National Endowment for the Arts grant.

1967 Receives Rockefeller grant.

1968 Marries Martha Speer; divorced 1975.

1969 *A Special Providence* published. *The Bridge at Remagen*, screenplay (co-written with William Roberts and Roger Hirson), released.

1971–72 Serves as Distinguished Writer-in-Residence, Wichita State University.

1975 *Disturbing the Peace* published. Receives grant from the National Institute of Arts and Letters.

1976 *The Easter Parade* published. Receives Rosenthal Foundation award.

1978 *A Good School* published. Receives National Magazine Award for short story "Oh, Joseph, I'm So Tired."

1981 *Liars in Love* published.

1982 Teaches creative writing at Boston University.

1984 *Young Hearts Crying* published. Receives National Endowment for the Arts award of $25,000. Teaches creative writing at Emerson College.

1985 *William Styron's "Lie Down in Darkness": A Screenplay* published.

1986 *Cold Spring Harbor* published.

1989 Teaches at University of Southern California.

1990–91 Teaches at University of Alabama at Tuscaloosa.

1992 Dies 7 November in Birmingham, Alabama.

old journalism converted into fiction by John O'Hara, novels and stories of manners by Mary McCarthy and John Cheever, and new imaginative social studies by Philip Roth and John Updike. Although the mission of these writers was being challenged by experimentalists holding a Coney Island mirror to the American self, many of the realists stayed on to record manners in clear (if not always plain) sentences.[3] Richard Yates belongs among his more famous contemporaries and elders of this sort, the ones who kept faith with the broad tradition of giving a general readership accessible accounts of American social experience.

Yates and His Contemporaries

At the time that he was first publishing, Yates worked some of the territory of America's best satirists. Roth's *Goodbye, Columbus,* published in 1959, was a book whose suburban scenes and varieties of middle-class types invite comparison with Yates's America; Roth's title story mocks the culture of abundance, playfully explores the ironies of Jewish assimilation, and rewards a child of the lower middle class with insights denied his privileged contemporaries. When Richard Yates wrote about Connecticut two years later in *Revolutionary Road* he avoided Roth's buffo and sustained caricature. While Roth piles on the comic effects, Yates uses bleak and pathetic details: *Goodbye, Columbus* mocks the middle-brow dopiness of Ron Patimkin, worshiper of Mantovani; *Revolutionary Road* tells us about the little white toy horse, taken from a bottle of Scotch, that April Wheeler's father gave his adoring daughter.

The targets of Roth's satire vociferously and piously objected to his narrow choice of subject—B'nai B'rith's Anti-Defamation League voiced these formal complaints, and he answered them with a harsher and even more specifically Jewish complaint of his own, *Portnoy's Complaint.* But Yates's net was cast so wide, his critique of middle-class desperation was so pervasive, that the entire American middle class, practically, would have had to come forward to object to the unflattering portraits. And those models—the lost people in the middle—would never be able to specify what, precisely, Yates had done to them. There were no comic shots, attacks on specific beliefs, ethnic slurs (real or even imagined); Yates's satire was directed at damaged souls, and that is what made his attacks dead on the mark.

Mary McCarthy also published satire in Yates's era—everything from send-ups of academe and transparent stories about real-life literary intellectuals to her 1960s best-seller about Vassar girls, *The Group.* This work explored a theme that she shared with Yates—the spectacle of well-educated people messing up their lives with warped ideas about personal authenticity and individualism. The treatment of the subject, however, shows how very different Yates was from a comic satirist with a bone to pick.

Columbia University in the 1950s is the intellectual backdrop for *Revolutionary Road:* Yates makes Frank Wheeler into a caricatured mouthpiece for certain key ideas that emanated from the university. Lionel Trilling's critique of middle-class liberal smugness and the rigidities of half-formed modern minds filters into the portrait of Frank, the character who criticizes living room Freudianism, mocks conformity, and calls, in the manner of Trilling, for reason and maturity. But the trouble is that Frank's apparent flexibility and rationality distort Trilling's way of questioning social pieties: Frank merely rationalizes his own inertia, submits to Revolutionary Road, and resorts to cheap Freudianism when it suits him to analyze his wife's depression and despair. He is the ideal type of the simplistic liberal, Trilling's favorite object of ironic analysis in *The Liberal Imagination.*[4]

Another Columbia figure of the era, the sociologist C. Wright Mills, analyzes the absurdities of the business world in his study *White Collar;* Frank Wheeler, good part-time radical that he is, would pay lip service to the ideas of Mills, the Marxist critic. Again, the difficulty is that Frank becomes immersed in contradictions, including the mindless life of the Knox Company, where he shuffles papers for a living. He comes to enjoy the routine of flirting with secretaries, writing factitious memos and promotional copy, and avoiding anything that smacks of thinking. A job is a place to turn off your mind and fantasize about large, vague plans.[5]

As an acute analyst of self-deception and illusions about enlightenment, Yates shares a great deal with McCarthy: she creates smart Vassar girls who outsmart themselves with crazy schemes for child rearing, mechanical approaches to sex and politics, and doctrinaire theories of how to lead the good life; he creates the wised-up and cool protagonist with an answer for everything and a plausible cliché about contemporary America to bolster his cynical arguments. Typically, however, McCarthy is sardonic and clear in her attacks: her portraits of the Group have caused real Vassar graduates to take offense, to complain about unfairness and misrepresentation, and to accuse McCarthy of personal attack.[6] In comparison, despite the biographical sources of his work, there's hardly anything vengeful in Yates's satire: his ridicule does not seem invested with the anger and mockery that one finds throughout McCarthy's work. Driven by the desire to expose types and states of mind rather than former acquaintances, Yates comes across as more disinterested. In point of fact, he is often quite literal in his use of details from life; yet his tendency to go over the ground of his parents' divorce and his unhappy childhood is more obsessional than denunciatory: he tells exemplary facts of his time rather than intimate secrets. His generalizing powers make him less involved than McCarthy with exposing individuals. Yates is interested in arranging patterns of dishonesty in his time.

Yates's subtle observation and presentation of the climate of his times bring to mind the world of John Cheever. Cheever and Yates both deal with illusion-filled strivers and cocktail party performers, but both writers refuse to flay their characters alive in the McCarthy manner: both extend understanding to their damaged people, while keeping a discreet distance from them. Cheever provokes a range of responses in a story such as "O Youth and Beauty!," a tale of a romantic miscalculator who thinks he can recapture his youth as a college track star by jumping over coffee tables at parties. Pathos, poignancy, mockery, melancholy, yearning: these responses enter the portrait of Cheever's doomed middle-aged man.

At his best, Yates can evoke similar responses—make us understand Frank the magnetic performer as a victim of tired, conventional older parents, April the depressive as a victim of high-flying, glamorous 1920s parents—and force us to see more than sardonic messages about flawed people. Like Cheever, he is unsettled in his attitudes and unwilling to use one mode to describe his characters. Once said, however, this is not meant to imply that Yates has the stylistic range of Cheever. Cheever's sentences are highly figurative; Yates's sentences, by contrast, never draw attention to themselves. On the level of form, Cheever is a writer of tales, at once in the tradition of Hawthorne in their weird and haunting emblematic quality while moving in the direction of postmodern experimentation.

Cheever's reports about suburban snobs always reach the reader in unusual packaging: sustaining conceits, such as using a swimmer's day as a vehicle to explore a community's values, and symbolic actions, usually extravagant or outrageous forms of behavior, are his modes for describing the pressures of life in the upper middle class. Yates's stories often read like case histories; they use details in a matter-of-fact manner; they weave the locutions of the characters into the descriptive prose as well as the dialogue; they live by a different conception of narration, a firm commitment to the language and thought patterns of ordinary people. Yates the teller refuses to outstrip his characters by employing a bravura style or a fantastic structure. In ignoring postmodernism and living in the stylistic past, he achieved an altogether different effect from most of his contemporaries and built a reputation that was far less glamorous than Kurt Vonnegut's or Joseph Heller's or Thomas Pynchon's.

Yates takes his place in a long tradition of social evaluation that has brought in evidence about the tyranny of social conventions, the smallness of American ambition, the blighting of hopes in a mass society, the burden of false individualism, and the loneliness built into democratic culture. The narrower places of the American spirit are Yates's territory. His more famous contemporaries who experimented with form could never content themselves with the limitations that Yates placed on himself; they ranged through realms, tore through time frames, broke down plausibilities in order to critique modern society. Yates worked out his vision of American distress without undergoing the stylistic and intellectual fire baptism of the 1960s: he bent language into no new shapes; he apparently cared little about R. D. Laing, aerospace, white negroes, the literature of the absurd, the theater of cruelty, or any other event or thought current that excited his bolder peers. They had their own flamboyant images of what was happening to the American spirit; he patiently believed in his set of devastating discoveries.

Yates's People

During a career that began in the 1950s and lasted until his death in 1992, Yates mapped out his own version of modern America, peopling it with men and women from the vulnerable yet never economically miserable regions of society, who suffer from diminishment of self, frustrated status yearning, and chronic social ineptitude. Yates's characters typically get through most of their lives without knowing what's wrong; Yates's readers are immersed in the elements that produce a failure. From his 1954 story of the crowd in a Queens bar, a group of men drifting into marriage, until *Cold Spring Harbor,* his 1986 novel about a Long Island family lost in its class pretensions, Yates focused on the ways his damaged adults and children never quite achieve fulfillment, recognition, and sustaining emotion.

All his life Yates admired F. Scott Fitzgerald: the green light at the end of the dock in *The Great Gatsby,* the promise of something glimmering and special just ahead, is one of his master themes; and yet Yates never seems to submit to the glamour and joy of American promise.[7] In his novels and stories he subtracts most of the romance from his people's lives, rewriting Fitzgerald's winter dreams of love and social ambition in a minor key. Yates's people are also almost always strugglers on their way to jobs in business rather than golden people at the country club. He adapts one of Fitzgerald's central conflicts—the glimpse of promise that can distort life—and transfers it to his own social world: he makes the pursuit of the glimmering prospect a matter of pathetic selves pursuing vanishing horizons.

Yates's damaged selves come in several varieties. There is April Wheeler in *Revolutionary Road,* perhaps Yates's most successfully rendered version of a collapsing identity. A highly attractive young woman with unfocused acting ambitions, she stumbles into marriage with sexy Frank Wheeler, another unformed New Yorker who talks brilliantly and can diagnose every social problem in the American 1950s but his own. After drifting to the suburbs for the benefit of their children, she takes up one of Frank's favorite themes: that there is something better elsewhere, perhaps in Europe or perhaps in the company of the right people. "I still had this idea that there was a whole world of marvelous golden people somewhere . . . Sort of heroic super-people, all of them beautiful and witty and calm and kind, and I always imagined that when I did find them I'd suddenly know that I belonged among them" (*RR,* 258). The pathos of these lines distills Yates's vision of April and the other severely diminished people in his books.

Another version of the damaged self is Gloria Drake in *Cold Spring Harbor,* the last in Yates's gallery of wretched and pretentious older women. A lonely single parent in the Greenwich Village of the 1940s, she fortifies herself with sherry and goes on and on in conversation with perfect strangers, expending her small fund of knowledge and dignity and making herself into a spectacle.

Another recurring figure is the youngish man who seems to wallow in his own failure. Walter Henderson, in *Eleven Kinds of Loneliness,* is highly skilled at losing games, failing college courses, and getting fired from jobs. The adult who has lost at the office is merely the latest version of the little boy who knew how to impress his playmates by falling down dead. "Nobody could match the abandon with which he flung his limp body down the hill, and he reveled in the small acclaim it won him." Other apparently young and vigorous men seem to relish their disordered lives: in *The Easter Parade* a Columbia instructor takes great pleasure in analyzing his ineffectual personality, and dismisses a compliant and pretty girl from his life because he prefers a year's worth of psychoanalysis to any immediate romance.

Social Imagination and Literary Heritage

Yates's understanding of collapse and loss of psychic wholeness can be connected to several strains in American social thought—to Alexis de Tocqueville writing about thwarted aspirations in a democracy; to a variety of nineteenth- and twentieth-century writers and critics who analyzed the deadening effects of our commercial culture; and to several social thinkers who described the terms of survival in a mass society. Yates's world of stunted selves has its intellectual roots in a famous chapter of Tocqueville's *Democracy in America:* "Why There Are So Many Men of Ambition in the United States But So Few Lofty Ambitions."[8] The conditions that produce Yates's characters are well described:

> But equality, though it gives every citizen some resources, prevents any from enjoying resources of great extent, and for this reason desires must be confined within fairly narrow limits. Hence in democracies ambition is both eager and constant, but in general it does not look very high. For the most part life is spent coveting small prizes within reach. It is not so much the small scale of their wealth as the constant and strenuous efforts needed to increase it, which chiefly diverts men in democracies from high ambitions. They strain their faculties to the utmost to achieve paltry results, and this quickly and inevitably limits their range of vision and circumscribes their powers. They could well be much poorer and yet be more magnanimous (Tocqueville, 629).

In another context Tocqueville fires off an epigram that distills the consequence of the above passage and brings many of Richard Yates's people into focus: "A mind cannot be gradually enlarged on like a house" (Tocqueville, 629). Tocqueville is here summing up the narrowness that he observed in the lives of many Americans who had compromised their desires and thwarted their own inclinations in early life in order to make money. Such people cannot thereafter will away or spend themselves out of the confines that have been established in their early years. Yates's people—Frank Wheeler working for the same business machine company his father sweated his life away in, the Grimes sisters in *The Easter Parade* living out the consequences of their parents' divorce—come straight out of Tocqueville's analysis. The destinies of his characters are altogether as confining as the prospects described in *Democracy in America.*

Again, a short passage from the French commentator helps to bring the vision of the American fiction writer into focus: this time Tocqueville is writing about the "inflexible" rules of advancement in a democracy that make it difficult "to reach a position of some importance quickly" (Tocqueville, 630). He describes the levels of frustration that we are soon to find in every one of Yates's books: all men

> are forced through the same sieve, and all without discrimination are made to pass a host of petty preliminary tests, wasting their youth and suffocating their imagination. So they come to despair of ever fully enjoying the good things proffered, and when at last they reach a position in which they could do something out of the ordinary, the taste for it has left them (Tocqueville, 630).

Exhausted from the rigors of advancement, Yates's characters wither spiritually in their suburban houses and New York apartments. At times they seem buried alive in petty concerns and inherited family problems that are like so many ugly heirlooms.

Tocqueville's sense of "despair of ever enjoying the good things" runs through the Gilded Age into the Great Depression, and Yates extends it through the seemingly buoyant years after World War II. He specializes in describing Americans ground down by the quiet, relentless demands of fitting into the affordable house and the office cubicle. One story in *Liars in Love,* "Oh, Joseph, I'm So Tired," has just the right title to express the lives of many Yates people: taken from a little Christmas play for children in which a worn-down woman plays the Virgin Mary, the title also has Yates's characteristic ironic tincture. Yates's contemporaries chose not to chronicle such inconspicuous defeats, favoring shock, sexual revelation, apocalypse, stylistic experiment, and rage as their hallmarks. Yates's America seems to harken back to the late nineteenth and early twentieth centuries, a time when the ordinary person felt the smallness of his or her destiny in relation to the seemingly invulnerable forces of the railroads and Wall Street. The spectacular fortunes and towering influences of big capitalists were matched by a smallness of mind, vulgarity of attitude, and falling off of romantic ambition that pervaded many lives.

In *A Piece of My Mind,* Edmund Wilson describes the ways in which such a social climate blighted the life of his father and his generation of idealistic professional men. In the 1880s Edmund Wilson Sr. contended with the depredations of a crassly commercial society: "The period after the Civil War—both banal in a bourgeois way and fantastic with gigantic fortunes—was a difficult one for Americans brought up in the older tradition . . . [they] had to deal with a world in which the kind of education and the kind of ideals it served no longer really counted for much."[9] A cultivated and public-spirited figure who thought of politics in "classical republican terms," Wilson's father had to compromise so much of himself that he wound up a neurasthenic victim of the times, a brilliant lawyer reduced to serving the railroad interests, and forgetting the destiny that he had conceived for himself in his youth. The son describes the "neurotic eclipses" that punctuated the father's entire adult life: the very phrase seems to sum up the lives of many real people and fictional creations who were conspicuous between the 1880s and the 1930s (Wilson, 214). Their fates were tragic or pathetic, compromised by grand misfortunes or by routine misunderstandings in a booming commercial society.

Wilson's father's situation—the "dizzying temptations, overpowering pressures, insidious diversions of purpose" of the Gilded Age—leads us to other such misunderstandings of post–Civil War America (Wilson, 214). Our literature that deals with the palmy days of business expansion before the Great Depression is crowded with people who stood to the side—or were pushed to the side. The cast of diminished people in fiction includes a variety of social types, all of whom share in the more depressing aspects of American prosperity and self-confidence: their manners or backgrounds or sensibilities disqualify them for the rough and tumble of getting money and throwing it around.

A variety of victims in fiction comes to mind: Edith Wharton's Lily Bart in *The House of Mirth*, a finely tuned but fragile nature dragged down by exposure to the vulgar rich and as a consequence stripped of the dignity she possessed as a young girl; Henry James's susceptible protagonist in "The Jolly Corner," haunted by a brutal image of capitalism, a specter that literally pursues him in his Gramercy Park mansion; Theodore Dreiser's Hurstwood in *Sister Carrie*, an unstable romantic who misunderstands the savage terms of American business; Ernest Hemingway's Krebs in "Soldier's Home," a young man so damaged by the spirit of patriotism and go-getting that he sinks into inertia. These characters fall apart in the period of America's greatest expansion and optimism. They need no Great Depression in order to collapse: the ingredients of big money, fast-track competition, and loud rhetoric about progress are enough to contribute to their inner losses and social failures.

In a later period of prosperity Richard Yates created his own assortment of personalities disordered by a noisy and insistent culture of optimism, money-getting, and social climbing. The 1950s are Yates's crucial decade, the period when his talent took shape and his vision of America crystallized. Although the depression and the war years are important backdrops in several of his works, the 1950s provide the smoldering discontent, the inertia, and the frustration that fuel Yates's imagination. Without the thinly veiled meanness of many of Senator Joseph McCarthy's supporters in the general public, a story such as "The B.A.R. Man"—about the suppressed rage of a Queens veteran—would be impossible; without the contrast between suburban colonial quaintness and Levittown uniformity, *Revolutionary Road* would lack its peculiarly deadening atmosphere; without the burgeoning advertising, public relations, and computer businesses, many Yates characters would not have the right settings against which to whine and rage; without the context of TV's cant about family happiness and its ludicrous backdrop of daytime cartoons, Yates's people would lose their ironic impact.

Reading Yates's work is like reliving arid stretches of the postwar years, but reliving them through the eyes of a brilliantly selective observer. The reader gets just the right details of a bleak day at the office, an evening at a cheap suburban roadhouse, a Sunday afternoon with guests droning on about politics, a stifling Friday night when the husband wants to drink with the boys and the wife wants to see a Gregory Peck picture.

Diminishment

Yates's books are charged by the period in which Americans had small-scale ambitions and yet a vague sense that perhaps there were bigger prizes and satisfactions somewhere just ahead. David Riesman's *The Lonely Crowd* provides the reader of Yates with a vantage point on the goals and expectations of people in the 1950s. Riesman's "other-directed" person tends to become "his succession of roles and encounters and hence to doubt who he is or where he is going."[10] Yates's men and women emerge from this picture of social character: unlike the clear-headed strivers of an older America, they do not look to a definable goal—a star, as Riesman puts it—of business or professional success. "A Milky Way" of possibilities—sometimes the vague hopes of the lower middle class, sometimes the impractical dreams about art and literature of the educated bourgeoisie—blurs the course of their lives and makes

them seem insubstantial as people. Yates's works are crowded with characters who have lost the connecting threads of their lives and drift from
role to unconvincing role. In pursuit of happiness, they are willing to try
on any career or love affair that might feed their yearnings.

Eleven Kinds of Loneliness, Yates's gallery of midcentury lives, is a succession of losses sustained by people who hardly seem aware of what is happening to them.[11] They doubt their role of the moment and become confused about the next step. Vincent Sabella, a traumatized city kid thrown
by the welfare system into a suburban school, is a typical baffled self. Trying to fake a middle-class identity and be one of the kids, he buries himself in his own lies and ineptitude, finally sinking into savage resentment
of his well-intentioned young teacher. A gentlemanly businessman like
Walter Henderson also fakes his way into a total collapse. The book is
rich in insubstantiality. The wife of a long-term TB patient in a story
called "No Pain Whatsoever" is poignantly shown in several false positions: she is observed having to manufacture soothing bedside conversation for her unresponsive husband in the hospital during the Christmas
season. Just before this scene, she has had to fend off the vulgar advances
of a boyfriend who seems like a desperate solution to her loneliness. After
leaving the hospital, she assumes an additional uncomfortable role—
being "in command": "Finally it was over, or nearly over; she managed to
control her shoulders, to blow her nose and put her handkerchief away,
closing her bag with a reassuring, businesslike snap" (*11K,* 72).

Yates's 1950s characters watch the best of themselves slip away as
they settle for false recognitions, evasions, anger, and the pleasures of
defeat. Not knowing very clearly what they want, they seem to take
whatever their current social environment has to offer. David Riesman's
recurring theme—that we Americans look for signals from peers instead
of cultivating strong personal convictions—is ubiquitous in Yates. The
stories and novels are filled with promises made by bosses, sergeants,
husbands, teachers: those who listen are shown struggling to figure out
what went wrong. In "Jody Rolled the Bones" an army unit is brutally
let down when their sergeant, with little apparent warning, leaves them
without any visible show of regret. In "Fun with a Stranger" a group of
schoolchildren are humiliated by a life-denying teacher who they believe
will come through with a Christmas treat: careful watchers of signals,
the children imagine that a pile of red and white packages contains good
things. When each child unwraps a 10-cent eraser, the effect is immediate and total embarrassment. The narrator simply comments that "there
would be no need to think about any of it anymore" (*11K,* 125).

Class

Besides his victims Yates also has his dreamers, status-hungry middle-class people who try to work out larger-than-average destinies for themselves. Status seeking almost always foreshadows disappointment or disaster: the people become pathetic cases, usually crazy, broke, and baffled. In Yates's America, unlike Fitzgerald's, the pleasures of snobbery and material possession vanish quickly. No one really gets to savor moving upward, which is a strange circumstance in the work of a writer who is almost constantly focusing on class, prestige, and power. Yates cuts the good life and stylishness down to size, reducing them to routines, pretentious rhetoric, and false management of impressions. Like Fitzgerald or John O'Hara, he interrogates the terms of classiness, but unlike them, he paints his stark picture of a class-ridden society without indulging in cautionary messages. Characteristically, one of his people will complain about some class injury or offense—and the narrator will say nothing.

Almost every Yates work has its overreaching snob, artist manqué, or intellectual pretender: if not Frank Wheeler looking down at the middle class from his pseudointellectual's point of view, then the mother in *A Special Providence* with her airs and her complacency about her position, her entitlements, and the special destiny in store for her son. Class consciousness and elitism are luxuriant growths that Yates studies in many forms. He wants to know their manifestations, among roommates, hospital patients, and Westchester professionals, and he also wants to study their origins, in the family and in institutions. How have Americans been carefully taught to be different and better than their neighbors? How do we find ourselves in a society where democratic niceness is a mere pretense, and the pretentiousness of class feeling is the reality?

The triad of gender, race, and class has come to occupy a central position in literary criticism in the 1990s: Yates's work provides a rich resource for explorers of the third topic. He takes his place beside a small group of contemporaries—John Cheever and Mary McCarthy on the middle classes, Louis Auchincloss on the stratospheric old money types, Raymond Carver on the suffering blue collar people—who excelled at studying antidemocratic America. Neither a Marxist nor a mandarin, nor an upper-class surveyor of our society, Yates approaches class consciousness from the vantage point of his shaky and rather insecure position in the middle class.[12] Never sure about money or educational credentials or family background in his own life, he created scores of characters who display their class anxieties and yearnings—what the sociologist C. Wright Mills calls "status panic."[13]

Yates used a number of configurations to show Americans facing the inexorable fact of social difference: an upper-class wife clashing with a middle-class husband in *Young Hearts Crying,* a working-class boyfriend judged by a college-educated woman in *Eleven Kinds of Loneliness,* older women worried about the perceptions of well-to-do neighbors in *The Easter Parade* and *Cold Spring Harbor,* prep school boys without the right tweed jackets in *A Good School.* The list should also include those whose anxieties and pretensions involve artistic and literary goals rather than social status: a pathetic cabby who wants to tell his life story, an unsuccessful sculptress, a cheeky employee of a labor newspaper who fancies himself a Walter Winchell. At times these misconceived fantasies seem like Ralph Kramden's schemes from *The Honeymooners* turned tragic.

For an equally comprehensive picture of class in America the reader of fiction would have to go back to O'Hara, whose tales of swells and climbers, the secure and the edgy, are cluttered with masterful and detailed accounts of class-ridden characters challenged by new and different people and threatening changes in social values. Julian English, O'Hara's glamour boy and member of the established upper class in *Appointment In Samarra,* is losing his footing in Gibbsville, Pennsylvania, at the beginning of the Great Depression: in scene after scene he falls from grace with the local powers that be, especially the Irish Catholics who are moving in at the country club. O'Hara's study of panic presages Yates's books about slipping and stumbling on the road to being socially secure. Yates rewrites O'Hara's stories of catastrophe, using the materials of his era and also several new ideas about society that were not as relevant to O'Hara's world. O'Hara's snobs and bullies and climbers are contending with class anxiety, of course, but they are essentially people of the first third of the century, which is to say those unaffected by postmodern technology, radical changes in public deportment, and new pressures coming from mass society. Class and status are treated less romantically by a writer who has lived his youth in an age of TV and public relations. O'Hara wrote about local big shots cut down by fate and changing public opinion; Yates wrote about smaller people who are the victims of post–World War II conventions and vaguer, more insidious forces—not the hostile neighbors so much as the menacing culture of conformity.

Yates's vision of class in America bears a marked resemblance to the ideas of C. Wright Mills, the Marxist-oriented sociologist who studied esteem and class in *The Power Elite* and *White Collar,* and Erving Goffman, the social theoretician who invented the study of performance and impression management in his landmark work *The Presentation of Self in Everyday Life.*

White Collar is an invaluable source book for the student of Yates. Several of its major ideas provide a framework for viewing the lonely and confused people in Yates's fiction. There is a form of status panic that Mills describes as emerging from "status proletarianization": by this he is referring to the loss of prestige and esteem that white-collar workers have sustained during the mid-twentieth century (Mills, 295–98). Once held in considerable regard by employers and the community, white-collar workers of the 1940s and 1950s had been slipping into a precarious social position. Their educations did not count for much in a workplace that increasingly valued routine, rationalization, and efficiency. Their often college-trained minds were uneasy with many of the demands of business. White-collar workers also experienced considerable anxiety because there was nothing in their lives to depend on for defining identity but a job. Mills leads us right to Yates's fiction as he describes all the tension connected with explaining one's role. Since the job usually is none too attractive as an indicator, the white collar workers make the elaborate excuses or use the clever distancing that we find in the portrait of Frank Wheeler in *Revolutionary Road.*[14] A job, if we listen to these workers, is really, well, nothing. Mills also argues that his office people claim higher status in a different locale or at a different time.

The "If-you-knew-me-where-or-when" ploy leads directly into Yates's world of dreamers and white-liars. Frank Wheeler—man of the world and free spirit, living room philosopher and cosmopolitan—is merely working at a business machine company because he has a family and because he has a cavalier attitude toward that rather petty thing called a career. As he talks his way out of the embarrassment of his dull job, he becomes a sign of his times, one of Mills's victims transformed into a complex being by Yates's subtle rendering.

Performance

Yates's 1950s vision of social class also corresponds to Erving Goffman's ideas of social performance. In analyzing the underlying structure of public behavior—how people make impressions, what routines they follow in projecting themselves—Goffman draws a floorplan of Yates's America. Fundamental to both writers' views of modern social presentation is the idea of the self as a "dramatic effect."[15] This phrase of Goffman's conveys the notion of the modern self as something other than a thing possessed; the self in action is instead a series of impressions made on an audience. People are pegs on which many manufactured and changing acts will eventually hang. It follows that status is also not a permanent possession but a string of actions that need to be embellished by settings, clothes, and opinions. Yates's people emerge from the same theatrically conceived view of self and social performance.

Rejecting the Freudianism of his era, Yates works on effects rather than causes, external manifestations rather than deep motives. In his best work he gives vivid form to Goffman's major premise that the order of society is maintained by dramatic gestures, impression management, face saving, and the avoidance of "inopportune intrusions" (Goffman 1959, 209). Yates's novels and stories bring Goffman's abstract formulations into the concrete realms of post–World War II America. Performing self Frank Wheeler—with his "terrifically sexy walk," his veneer of literary culture, and his cool manner—actually practices dramatic lines for the ride home with his wife, for an evening in the living room, for a morning at the office. He constantly rehearses speeches, goes over the steps of projecting himself, and even when communing with himself, he sets up a theatrical line, including a physical setting that highlights his positive attributes, and a series of gestures that make him superior to his circumstances. After the disastrous opening of *Revolutionary Road,* a scene in which April Wheeler fails miserably in a performance of *The Petrified Forest* at the Laurel Players' little theater, Frank drives home filled with the spirit of Goffman's performing self:

> With a confident, fluid grace he steered the car out of the bouncing side road and into the hard clean straightaway of Route Twelve, feeling that his attitude was on a solid ground at last. A refreshing wind rushed in to ruffle his shirt and cool his brains, and he began to see the fiasco of the Laurel Players in its true perspective. It simply wasn't worth feeling bad about. Intelligent, thinking people could take things like this in their stride, just as they took the larger absurdities of deadly dull jobs in the city and deadly dull homes in the suburbs. Economic circumstances might force you to live in this environment, but the important thing was to keep from being contaminated. The important thing, always, was to remember who you were (*RR,* 20).

"Who you were" leads Frank to other theatrical settings and remembrances of past performances. "In his early twenties wearing the proud mantles of 'veteran' and 'intellectual' as bravely as he wore his carefully aged tweed jacket and washed out khakis": such phrases all but constitute the man's nature (*RR,* 20–21). Reactions to him ("men, and intelligent men at that, could actually want to hear him talk") and evaluations of his own showmanship ("there was nothing average about his performance in the beery, all-night talks that had begun to form around him") are the core of his being (*RR,* 21). Just as Goffman speaks of the self's putting together bits and pieces of available reality and fashioning a successful performance, Yates writes of Frank's assemblage of his past: "Loose strands of his character—the very traits that kept him dreaming and lonely among schoolboys and later among soldiers—these seemed suddenly to have coalesced into a substantial and attractive whole" (*RR,* 21).[16]

Wheeler is one among many Yates characters who live by routines, props, frantically rearranged scenery, and rehearsed dialogue. Nevertheless, mere phoniness is not the theme of either Goffman or Yates: working with the facts of social survival, both writers deal with low-level deception only incidentally. Their fundamental concern is the struggling social self, and ridicule and social satire are thus only incidental to their work. The "how" of impression management, rather than its morality, is the central concern in Goffman and Yates. Because of this fascination with strategy as opposed to value judgment, neither writer has engaged a very large audience: subtle, analytic, and lacking in flashy presentation, such writers chart the effects of the everyday American self without attempting to thrust their persona before the public. They prefer to analyze histrionic types rather than join them. In *Eleven Kinds of Loneliness* Yates shows how his character Leon Sobel embellishes an abysmal performance as a writer for *The Labor Leader* by giving himself a column called "Sobel Speaking," by falling into a silly and semiliterate personal style (a breeziness mocked by E. B. White in *The Elements of Style* as properly belonging to rank amateur writers in the "Class Notes" sections of alumni magazines), and even by trying to make a stubbornly unfashionable rainhat look like something from *The Front Page.*

The thwarted status yearning and energetic impression management of Yates's characters lead to an array of embarrassments, misfires, and catastrophes. From his earliest stories to his last novel, *Cold Spring Harbor,* Yates follows the careers of men and women who tangle the gears of contemporary America, who break one of the middle rungs of the social or corporate ladder, who stumble in a country of opportunity. While not precisely born losers, his inept people bear the marks of woe associated with the permanently clumsy: they explain themselves too much, display their vulnerabilities, and habitually play up to a world that repulses them.

Yates's America is filled with people trying to play the game and as often as not failing. Stories from the 1978 volume *Liars in Love* sweep across the decades from the Roosevelt years to the 1970s and show Americans mishandling their jobs and miscalculating their prospects. The opening story, "Oh, Joseph, I'm So Tired," is a study of the ways in which a pretentious Greenwich Village sculptress of the New Deal period overestimates her talent, humiliates herself, and proceeds to vent her disappointments on an innocent minor figure in her life.

In another book from Yates's later career, *Young Hearts Crying*, the protagonist, Harvard-educated Michael Davenport, is a more fully developed version of the discredited self.[17] Davenport loses social and professional ground in the 1950s and 1960s while his bohemian friends do well in the arts. He is dragged down by some mysterious under-tow—perhaps his marriage to a self-centered rich girl, perhaps his naive evaluation of the demands of the New York arts scene, perhaps his essentially adolescent, dreamy view of a career. He comes off badly, whether trying to be a solid suburbanite or maintaining a friendship with a painter who exhibits at the Museum of Modern Art. As a renter in Larchmont, he is compared to Dagwood Bumstead by his sophisti-cated artist friend Tom Nelson. When a guest at the Nelsons', he becomes so inappropriately overinvolved with Nelson's beautiful, hand-crafted toy soldiers that he pulls up a carpet to make room for play and earns a curt correction from his hostess. Michael and Lucy Davenport are models of how-it-shouldn't-be-done; the unwritten social prohibi-tions of their society bedevil and destroy them.

Yates's young hearts cry for professional success, friends, and the excitements of New York life after World War II. Michael and Lucy characteristically haunt the White Horse Tavern in Greenwich Village during the 1950s, but never realize it to be the hangout of Dylan Thomas until his nightly presence there is mentioned in his obituary. Their situation is once again best understood by one of Goffman's insights in *The Presentation of Self in Everyday Life,* the concept of "defini-tional disruption" (Goffman 1959, 13, 141). When Davenport or Frank Wheeler or the pathetic and pretentious mother Pookie in *The Easter Parade* define themselves, there is always some person or contradictory circumstance that cuts them down. A half-crazed neighbor can ask an embarrassing question in the middle of Frank's swaggering discourse about contemporary America. Pookie and the other older women generally have some defect in their dress or makeup; often their speech is slurred from drinking. They wind up redefined by their audience and by the reader.

But Yates is after much more than making his people into spectacles: his fiction draws attention to the meagerness of the expressive equipment at the disposal of his characters; in a society where class and status count for so much, where money and family standing determine people's life chances, the middle-middle class rarely seems to have the right setting, appearance, manners, and highlighting of actions to get very far. People born in the middle enter democracy's race for happiness with illusions rather than equipment.

Yates is one of a number of important writers who have studied the uncomfortable lives of the middle classes: neither shining from upper-class upbringings nor scowling because of the grosser forms of economic injustice, Yates's characters assume a position alongside Cheever's marginal people in Shady Hill, O'Hara's rejects and also-rans, the gauche and ill-prepared in our literature, including James's Daisy Miller. Taken together, these characters express an attitude in American literary culture that is neither romantic nor rebellious. Generally they are resigned rather than furious; they stew in their own juices rather than protest. Many of Cheever's wage-earning commuters contemplate their meager prospects as they stand on the margins of upper-middle-class society; some, like Johnny Hake in "The Housebreaker of Shady Hill," have used up the resources of their genteel upbringings and fallen into disrepute. They are too conventional in outward appearance and responses to be misfits, too compliant on the job or in the neighborhood to be rebels. They seem to exist in a limbo of accidents and bad timing.

Yates's rejected and discredited characters of course come perilously close to being the born losers and victims of raw naturalistic fiction; yet at his best, he transcends the merely deterministic and achieves a vision of people's social survival, the complexity of the struggle to stay afloat in American society. He uses his career to study the terms of enduring as well as the specification for total catastrophe. Among his tools as an artist are a gift for surprising plot twists, including just about every social mishap and inappropriate action that a middle-class person can fall prey to. His characters, most of them fairly sanguine in attitude, propel themselves toward destinies that are neither dully predictable nor fanciful.

While the creator of such an uncompromising vision of society was single-minded in his devotion to writing, he too stumbled into midcentury American life without the conventional equipment to achieve happiness.

Chapter 2
The Life of Richard Yates

Richard Yates wrote no autobiography, no memoirs; his only published essay about his past described the literary influences on his work. In interviews, too, he tended to deflect personal questions. But his fiction was so firmly rooted in his life that his biography can be deduced from patterns that recur in novel after novel and story after story.

When asked who was the model for Madame Bovary, Flaubert replied, "Emma Bovary, c'est moi." His acknowledged acolyte Richard Yates unconsciously and less elegantly paraphrased that famous remark when asked about the origins of his own female protagonist, Emily Grimes. *The Easter Parade,* he told a female admirer, is "my autobiography, sweetheart, Emily fucking Grimes is me, but I'm not saying I'm a cross-dressing creep or a damn homo . . . or well . . . maybe I am."[1]

"Emma Bovary, c'est moi" differs from "sweetheart, Emily fucking Grimes is me" in style alone: Yates translates Flaubert's precise elegance into his own characteristically juicy mid-twentieth-century American idiom. Even among his fellow writers, Yates was almost obsessively diligent in finding the exact words he wanted—his colleague Jayne Anne Phillips called him "the consummate perfectionist" (*RY,* 41). Other eulogists at Yates's memorial service spoke of his perfectionism, several of them coupling it with his honesty, almost as if those two qualities were one and the same: his friend E. Barrett Prettyman Jr. spoke of Yates's "total integrity. He never compromised with less than the perfect word, nor with less than the total truth" (*RY,* 43).

Driven as he was by the *mot juste,* Yates nevertheless avoided describing his art, because to do so would have compelled him to call himself an artist, a title he fiercely resisted. He was comfortable thinking of himself as a craftsman, arriving at large truths about his culture by recording the stray bits of action and speech that most of us ignore. The snippet about Emily Grimes quoted above is pure Yates dialogue: embarrassed to confess that Emily Grimes's features could be formed out of his own masculine clay, yet clearly proud of his accomplishment in doing so, Yates distances himself from his questioner by addressing her with a Bogart-like "sweetheart," interpolates the all-purpose GI intensifying adjective into the name of a character he loves and admires, and belligerently denies identifying with transvestites or gays. And then in the next breath, doubling back on his truculent position, he reveals the insecurity behind the macho pose.

The snippet also typifies Yates characters' speech, which falls into the same steady patterns from character to character and book to book. Yates's characters generally share his speech patterns, his social insights, his extreme self-consciousness. In some works he varied important details of their personal histories—Emily Grimes's sex, obviously, and less obviously, the secure middle-class upbringings of Frank Wheeler and Michael Davenport. But Frank and Michael and Emily's boyfriends all address women as "sweetheart" (and "baby" and "honey" and "dear"), and they all share certain verbal tics, physical mannerisms, and attitudes with each other and with Yates. "There's plenty of myself in that book," Yates said of *Revolutionary Road.* "Every character in the book was partially based on myself, or on some aspect of myself."[2]

Yates felt limited to two modes: he could write about his own experience explicitly, changing names and minor details, which he did in such works as *A Special Providence* and *A Good School,* or he could write about those same experiences implicitly and make marginally greater changes, as he did in *Revolutionary Road* and *Eleven Kinds of Loneliness.* What he could not do, because it would have seemed somehow dishonest or lazy, would have been to describe some purely imaginary situation and speculate on some theoretical protagonist's possible reactions to his imaginary scenario. "I can read hardly any of the . . . new 'post-realists,' " he complained in 1972, dismissing such then-trendy authors as Donald Barthelme and John Barth. Postrealist fiction, to his mind, tended to ignore emotional problems in favor of intellectual puzzles; postrealist writers saw themselves not as chroniclers of the contemporary scene but as "fictionists," technical innovators in a long literary tradition, on which their work commented and to which it often alluded (Henry, 76). Their subject was primarily their work, and it concerned fiction and ideas instead of people and their lives.

Yates was offended especially by the idea that life had become suddenly too complicated or incomprehensible somehow to be rendered in traditional ways. Life had always been complex, he fulminated, but his trendier contemporaries were too lazy to make sense of it now. When he would be criticized for repeating plots or characters or themes, he could take solace in F. Scott Fitzgerald's complaint against critics who urged him to write about newer subjects in newer styles: "Mostly, we

authors repeat ourselves—that's the truth . . . we learn our trade, well
or less well, and we tell our two or three stories—each time in a new
disguise—maybe ten times, maybe a hundred, as long as people will
listen."[3]

Yates's Childhood

Raised in an artist's home where human pleasures were routinely sacri-
ficed for such abstract concepts as Art and Beauty (with precious little
art or beauty abounding for all the sacrifice), Yates mistrusted abstract
ideas all his life and, taking Fitzgerald's advice to heart, examined
closely those few truths that had appeared plainly to him.

The recurring situations in Yates's fiction were identical to those that
formed his life. His father, described accurately in the foreword and
afterword of the novel *A Good School,* was a salesman for General Electric's Mazda lamp division named Vincent Matthew Yates, known as
"Mike," who divorced Richard's mother in 1929. He left the upbringing
of Richard, who was three years old, and Richard's seven-year-old sister,
Ruth, to their mother.

The divided family continued living in the New York metropolitan
area, and the Yates children saw their father regularly and depended on
him economically. Richard Yates's mother, Ruth Maurer Yates, wanted
to sculpt, and she devoted much of her energy toward that goal after the
divorce, energy that Yates later came to feel could more usefully have
been devoted to himself and his sister. Mostly, he came to resent his
mother's diversions of money to underwrite her sculpting career. He
sympathized with his father's complaints throughout the 1930s that
neither the depressed economy nor their own lower-middle-class status
allowed her the self-indulgence of a career in art.

Ruth Maurer Yates had attended various art schools—in Ohio
(where she was born), in New York City (at the Art Students League,
the Grand Central Art School, and with José De Creeft), and in Paris
briefly—but seems to have had extremely limited success as a sculptor.[4]
The high point of her artistic career was probably sculpting a bust of
President Franklin Roosevelt, which she presented to him at the White
House in 1933, a tale Richard Yates recorded in "Oh, Joseph, I'm So
Tired" forty-five years later.[5] Despite her lifelong insistence that her
career was about to yield tangible results, as Yates takes pains to point
out in the story, such triumphs earned her little recognition as an artist
and less money as a parent.

She served as president of the National Association of Women Artists and as chairman of the Fine Arts Federation of New York's committee to create an art gallery in City Center. (Later, she was appointed director of the gallery.) Rarely paying a living wage, these positions were more suitable for an artist of independent means than a working mother, but Ruth Maurer Yates felt the prestige would benefit her career and ultimately her family.

Her artistic career dominated Richard's youth and shaped his own strong opinions forcefully, both in opposition to his "poor pretentious mother," as he described her, and in admiration for her dedication to her art (*RY,* 22). Richard could have easily understood and forgiven and even continued to admire his mother for living a bohemian life, but she was bohemian only in that she was an artist and poor and lived in Greenwich Village. In her own mind, those facts were temporary and illusory: she would tell anyone who would listen that her values were patrician.

Although her sculpting did drain Ruth Yates's time from her children and her earning capacity, Richard admired her, especially when he was very young. She would comfort him with romantic stories to minimize their poverty: the future would be bright, she might say, or God would look out for them, or in a more pragmatic mood, she might confide that some wealthy art lovers were considering buying several pieces of her sculpture and the family might be well off very soon. But these visions never materialized, and he had to reconcile his mother's airy stories with the realization that she actually preferred deceiving herself to recognizing the truth around her.

When Yates got into his teens, his education became an issue his parents fought over bitterly. His mother insisted that her son attend a New England prep school, while his father argued that there was no money available to pay for such a wild extravagance. Ruth Maurer Yates won the argument, largely by getting a Connecticut prep school to agree to a reduced tuition for Richard and by shaming her ex-husband into paying that reduced fee. In 1942, while Richard was attending Avon Old Farms School, his 52-year-old father died. Richard was 16 at the time, and may well have felt that the added strain of paying for his education had caused his father's early death. Certainly from that point on, with the buttress of his family's money-earning potential gone, Richard was pressed to serve in his father's role as family breadwinner.

After graduating from the Avon School in 1944, Yates, like his character Bobby Prentice in *A Special Providence,* was drafted into the army. As terrifying and as boring as Yates described it in *A Special Providence,* the war did give him a notion that he might have a fate apart from his mother's. (The title *A Special Providence* is taken from a catchphrase of Prentice's mother, who believes that a special providence will look out for her family, but by that novel's end, it almost seems to apply to that unearthly power that will someday separate Prentice from his clinging mother.)[6] When the war was over, Yates, who fought without particular distinction in Belgium and France, returned to find his mother in her usual financial straits. He took a job rewriting copy for the United Press (like William Grove, his fictional counterpart in *A Good School,* he had edited the school paper at prep school) and, almost exactly as he describes Grove's postwar years in "Regards at Home," he got married in 1949, at least in part to get out of his mother's household.

Breaking Free from Mother

Yates's portraits of his mother incorporate sympathy with resentment. For decades he reacted to her just like a furious adolescent, realizing anew every time he wrote of her that scathing ridicule was his only protection against her foolish, self-contradictory fantasies. This relationship trained Yates, in life and in his fiction, to expose the hypocrisy of others, but because he also identified with his mother, he learned to question his own sincerity, forcing him to look deeply into superficially simple problems. Yates explained his preference for fiction without villains: "If you can blame everything on one of the characters in the story, then where's the weight of the story? . . . I much prefer the kind of story where the reader is left wondering who to blame until it begins to dawn on him (the reader) that he must bear some of the responsibility because he's human and therefore infinitely fallible" (Henry, 68–69).

He was reluctant to disparage either his self-absorbed mother or his absent father for any fault in parenting: even when a *Los Angeles Times* reporter asked him a painfully obvious question, he refused to give the obvious answer: "Asked if his childhood was happy, he says: 'Most people looking back believe their childhood was more poignant than anyone else's. So I won't compete for the poignancy prize. My parents were decent people. My childhood was OK.' "[7]

Yates's fiction more eloquently argues for an almost unrelievedly unhappy childhood and, when his childhood ended, a continuing feeling of oppression by his mother's selfishness. Even moving out of her home was insufficient to free him. After a few years of married life, with his first daughter born, Yates moved his family to Europe to escape his

mother and start his own artistic career. He had contracted lung problems in the army, and after being treated for tuberculosis following the
war, he received a disability pension on which he and his family traveled
to England and France in 1951. Some two years later, his wife took their
young daughter back to the United States, probably under conditions
somewhat less traumatic than those he described in the short story
"Liars in Love." As in that story, he and his wife were staying with her
English aunt until their constant quarreling and general discord finally
convinced Sheila Bryant Yates to return to America.

While in Europe, Yates lived alone in London, Antibes, and Cannes,
writing several drafts of at least two dozen short stories, and rejoined
his wife and daughter in 1953 in Redding, Connecticut, where she was
living with her mother and brother. Redding was a quiet suburb, and
far more posh than any area Yates had lived in until then. He seems
not to have enjoyed living in his mother-in-law's house—not surprisingly, especially in light of his difficult relationship with his own
mother—but the most disturbing (and artistically fortuitous) part of
their stay in Redding concerned Yates's brother-in-law, whose mental
problems served as a model for those of John Givings in *Revolutionary
Road*. (Yates's oldest daughter acknowledges matter-of-factly that
John Givings's mother, "Mrs. Givings, is my mother's mother," and
that "my uncle was half in and half out of the mental hospital at the
time.")[8] Yates moved the family to the less tony community of
Mahopac, in the Hudson Valley region of New York State, a move he
always regretted, according to his daughter, because he felt his daughters would have had advantages in that rich Connecticut town. Soon
after moving to Mahopac, Yates separated from his wife, and they
divorced in 1959.

Since his return from Europe, he had been earning a living ghostwrit-
ing articles published under the bylines of various executives for Rem-
ington Rand, "the business machines company that introduced the first
electronic computer, which was called the Univac," he recalled in 1981.
"All this was very boring stuff, but it only occupied about half of my
working life and so financed the whole of my first novel."[9]

Experience into Art

At the very start of the 1960s Yates's professional and personal lives
both changed radically: as soon as his marriage ended, his mother
became incapacitated by a massive cerebral hemorrhage, and his first

book had been accepted. When *Revolutionary Road* achieved favorable critical reviews and decent sales, new avenues opened up for Yates that had been blocked before. Universities offered him teaching positions, movie studios offered him screenwriting jobs, the Kennedy administration offered him a job writing speeches, foundations awarded him sizable cash grants, publishing companies offered him an anthology of short stories to edit, and most important, they offered to publish a collection of his early short stories, written before *Revolutionary Road*. The story collection came out in 1962 under the title *Eleven Kinds of Loneliness* and, like *Revolutionary Road,* was generally praised by critics and modestly accepted by the book-buying public.

Particularly satisfying was the admiration Yates's fellow writers lavished on the book. Dorothy Parker wrote in *Esquire* of "the sure perfection" of the stories, and decades and generations later, Ann Beattie wrote, "I know of no collection like it. Deservedly it has become a classic."[10]

What writers saw in *Eleven Kinds of Loneliness* was an artfulness that called no attention to itself. This *sprezzatura* was something Yates achieved quite deliberately, raised as he was by an artist who, much to Yates's embarrassment, exaggerated her artistic achievements wherever they existed and invented them where they did not. Asked if he felt his work had been unfairly neglected, he allowed that he did "in my more arrogant or petulant moments," but finally insisted on taking full responsibility for any neglect his work after *Revolutionary Road* and *Eleven Kinds of Loneliness* had received: "What happened after those two books was my own fault, nobody else's. If I'd followed them up with another good novel a few years later, and then another a few years after that, and so on, I might very well have begun to build the kind of reputation some successful writers enjoy" (Henry, 74).

Although his private correspondence and conversation often bubbled over with irritation about the publishing world's neglect of his work, he had learned from listening to his mother express similar frustrations to channel his own frustrations in a dignified way. Yates struggled to express in his work, too, the vexations of his own life in a way that reined in the confessional impulse. Blunt and well-written passages in his early drafts that directly blamed one person or one event were usually omitted from the final manuscript. Causality was always tricky, and Yates scrupulously sought to avoid the facile answers. Even when the easy answer seems correct, Yates at least entertains the more complex solution while conveying that complexity in a clear, supple, easy prose.

His style from the start was austere: based solidly on factual material, his fiction never explored for a paragraph the territory of the experimental, the metafictional, or the antifictional prose of the 1960s. He wrote plain sentences, used few metaphors, and most of all attached no grand scheme to the stories he told. His subject matter was determinedly his own. Just as he rejected Freudianism in favor of social observation, he had little patience with the concept that writers in need of subject matter should seek out adventures.

He urged the poet Maura Stanton, who was his student at Iowa in 1968, to write about her own experiences, however limited she felt they were. Only 22 years old, she had lived a fairly provincial life up to that point, but Yates coaxed her to remember some details about having been deeply in love once and, in her childhood, having visited a peculiar amusement park. With these fragments, he encouraged her to see that her life had been full of "great material" (*RY,* 49–51). The idea that writers needed to have bizarre experiences to write about offended Yates, as did most romantic notions.

Yates had colorful experiences, of course, but never in search of colorful material. Fighting in World War II, for example, was the result of being drafted, not of any urge for military glory. As Norman Mailer describes his fellow World War II soldiers, many had half-jokingly vowed to expose the army in a book after the war, and several did just that. Mailer himself, of course, and Gore Vidal, and Irwin Shaw, and John Horne Burns, and James Jones, and Herman Wouk, and a small army of other World War II veterans wrote realistic accounts of their military adventures in the years immediately following the war, and by the early 1960s most of them had written second and third volumes exposing flaws in postwar American society in a generally realistic and traditional style. Yates, having spent those 15 years teaching himself how to expose the truth in a plain style, was just starting to publish when a major change came over the American literary landscape.

Realism, the dominant literary mode of the postwar period, suddenly fell into disrepute. Yates's first two books had been written and published while realism was still fashionable, but by the time his third book, *A Special Providence,* came out in 1969, literary fashions had become everything Yates would not and could not be: hyperbolic, mystical, elaborate, pyrotechnical, academic, self-referential, literary, and worst of all, deliberately artistic. Yates blamed himself for not writing *A Special Providence* more quickly, but if he had written it at lightning speed, there's only a chance it might have been published before literary tastes flip-flopped. It was Yates's misfortune to perfect a realistic prose style just as realism was losing prestige and marketability, but within the confines of realism some new possibilities opened up after Yates's relative successes with *Revolutionary Road* and *Eleven Kinds of Loneliness.* In those two books, which he classified as only implicitly autobiographical, he had been striving for an objective voice. He had quite consciously tried to obey Flaubert's dictum, "The writer's relation to his work must be like that of God to the universe: omnipresent and invisible" (Henry, 70). This tropism away from explicitly autobiographical writing may have eased his troubled relationships with both his wife and his mother. But with his wife safely divorced from him now, and his mother institutionalized and unable to read his work, his personal cost in writing more explicitly autobiographical fiction was greatly reduced. While the literary firestorm raged all around him in the 1960s, with the trendier novelists broadening the frontiers of what fiction was and what it should be, Yates burrowed into his own past for his next book. He had written the first 10 stories in *Eleven Kinds of Loneliness* in the early 1950s, before *Revolutionary Road,* but he wrote the 11th story, "Builders," in 1961, as he described it, as "a direct autobiographical blowout [to] see if I could make decent fiction out of that. So as a sort of experimental warmup I wrote the story called 'Builders,' which was almost pure personal history, with a protagonist named Robert Prentice, who was clearly and nakedly myself. . . . Anyway, having done that, I felt I'd earned the right to extend the same kind of thing into a full-length novel, again with Robert Prentice as the protagonist" (Henry, 70).

Interruptions and Disturbances

In 1969 Yates published *A Special Providence,* a book about Prentice as a teenage infantryman in World War II abandoning his dependent artist manqué of a mother to fend for herself. *A Special Providence* was a failure both critically and commercially, and Yates later came close to disowning it. According to his publisher, he actually "wanted to delete the title from the card page" of his later books, "which lists other books by Richard Yates. He thought *A Special Providence* was badly written, badly edited, badly published" (*RY,* 59). In fact, it was mostly just badly timed.

By 1969 readers had been glutted by over two decades' worth of realistic, semiautobiographical World War II coming-of-age novels written by war veterans. Viewed alongside the competition in 1949, it might have read well, but readers in 1969 called for a glitzier subject than the ones Yates chose, or at least a more freewheeling style. The two phe-nomenally successful novels about World War II published in the 1960s, Joseph Heller's *Catch-22* and Kurt Vonnegut's *Slaughterhouse Five*, couldn't have contrasted more sharply in style and narrative technique with *A Special Providence*. Only ostensibly about World War II, Heller's and Vonnegut's flamboyant novels achieved great popularity in part because much of their thrust was savagely directed at (or could be easily applied to) the ongoing war in Vietnam and, more broadly, to general faults in contemporary American culture. Yates's aim, on the other hand, was much narrower: he tried to examine his troubled relationship with Ruth Maurer Yates and his own emerging values when he became independent of her. If Heller and Vonnegut were painting huge Hieronymus Bosch murals showing the horrors of war, Yates was seek-ing to paint a delicate miniature portrait of a boy and his mother against the backdrop of war. The times certainly promoted the more bravura attempts, and Yates accepted that judgment. Vonnegut, whom Yates met in the mid-1960s, became one of Yates's greatest admirers; despite a fundamentally different approach to fiction writing, the two enjoyed each other's work. Probably because of Vonnegut's unpretentious prose style, Yates singled him out for praise while uniformly blasting almost every other writer of experimental fiction.

Some of the reasons it took Yates seven years to write his third book were decidedly nonliterary: he drank heavily at times and, as he put it when confronted with a frank yes-or-no question, "I've been in and out of bughouses, yes," his longest stay being a three-month confinement in UCLA's Neuropsychiatric Institute in the summer of 1965.[11] Both the alcoholism and the mental illness played prominent roles in his next book, *Disturbing the Peace*. Like John Wilder in that novel, Yates drank excessively, especially as his marriage was breaking up, and was hospital-ized several times with psychiatric disorders, although it would be an error to read *Disturbing the Peace* as one of Yates's "explicitly" autobio-graphical accounts.

He based Wilder in large part on a Greenwich Village neighbor. Yates had returned to Manhattan when his first marriage broke up. In the early 1960s, when *Disturbing the Peace* is set, he was living a few blocks from where he had lived in Greenwich Village as a boy, and was teaching at the New School and at Columbia. There are obvious differences between Yates and Wilder—some physical (the six-foot-three Yates stresses Wilder's tininess), some economic (Wilder's par-ents owned a successful candy-manufacturing corporation), and some emotional (Wilder was a successful salesman, probably the least likely career for the shy, brooding Yates).[12] A minor character, Chester Pratt, portrayed as a malevolent presence in Wilder's life, interestingly enough, is in some ways closer to being a superficially explicit biographical analogue for Yates: Pratt is described as being a tall, thin speechwriter for Robert Kennedy.

Though Yates expressed a consistent contempt for literary fashions, *Disturbing the Peace* brought his interests together with one important postmodernist trend: the paradigm for the late 1960s and early 1970s was the metaphor of madness. Yates even discussed *Disturbing the Peace* in terms of that metaphor, in an uncharacteristic attempt to discuss the larger meaning of his work: "Maybe a man going crazy just might turn out to be a good metaphor for the Seventies. An appropriate metaphor" (Henry, 73). For a few years, at least, madness bore no stigma, and for some authors, such as Louis-Ferdinand Céline, having been institutionalized was merely another literary credential; along with Céline, who enjoyed his greatest readership in this period, films such as *King of Hearts,* which argues that the sanest members of society are locked up in mental institutions, and books such as Ken Kesey's *One Flew Over the Cuckoo's Nest,* with an identical theme, achieved cult status.

It was ironic that Yates, upholding the banner of realism, should be the writer of his generation who could describe a padded cell from the inside, because the message of Heller, Kesey, Vonnegut, et al. was that society was insane and should be shown as such. The one writer who did not think so was the one writer who knew what madness felt like. *Disturbing the Peace* tries to explore what the experience of being genuinely mad was like, but he took care not to overromanticize or, indeed, to romanticize it at all.

"I'd like to have the man go crazy without letting the book go crazy," Yates differentiated in 1972 (Henry, 74). (Still in the planning stages, *Disturbing the Peace* was to be a novel about a father stealing his son's girlfriend, which does not take place in the published novel.) Yates's avowed hostility to postmodern fiction notwithstanding, the end of *Disturbing the Peace* skirts near the edges of realism, for the only time in his writing career: deep into Wilder's psychotic delusion that the world's major media are broadcasting details of his mental breakdown, Yates's prose takes on, for a few pages, surrealist elements. These harrowing scenes are both successful and oddly comic, in a Joycean mode, suggesting that Yates might have done well to work in this mode more often than he did.

During this period, from the fall of 1964 through 1971, Yates taught at the prestigious Writer's Workshop at the University of Iowa. One of the most distinguished programs in the country, Iowa's graduate creative writing program would give Yates a light enough teaching load to let him write fiction. Yates complained privately about the low salary—under a thousand dollars a month—and felt that he would be able to survive only by writing Hollywood scripts over the summer breaks. Two months after arriving in Iowa City, he wrote his agent, "It becomes increasingly clear that screenwriting is the only way I can ever hope to achieve minimal solvency and still have the freedom to write fiction."[13] Still, with screenwriting positions being sporadic, teaching provided a stable source of income for Yates; since his job description included writing fiction and serving as a role model to his students, it was in many ways an ideal job for a writer, especially one without degrees or formal credentials. "Besides—" as his character Jack Flanders explains an identical offer in *The Easter Parade*, "oh, I know this sounds dumb, but it's kind of an honor to be invited out there."[14] Yates's seven-year stay at Iowa, the longest stretch of time he ever taught at any institution, ended when he was turned down for tenure, much to his surprise and his fury.

A Productive Decade

Yates continued to receive various awards—a grant from the National Institute of Arts in 1975, the year *Disturbing the Peace* was published, another the next year, when *The Easter Parade* came out, and a National Magazine Award in 1978 when *A Good School* was printed. But most of Yates's support in the years after failing to gain tenure at Iowa was in the form of a series of consecutive monthly payments of $1,500, paid to him by Delacorte Press (and later Houghton Mifflin) from 1973 through the early 1990s. Seymour Lawrence, an editor who had helped Yates publish his story "Jody Rolled the Bones" in the *Atlantic Monthly* in 1953 and who now had his own imprint, contracted to pay Yates this "kind of salary," as Lawrence put it, and Yates responded with his most productive period: in the 10 years between 1975 and 1984, Yates published over half of his life's work (*RY*, 59).

This period began inauspiciously: Yates's New York City apartment caught fire in 1976, causing the writer to be hospitalized with serious burns. He spent a month in bed being treated for his burns. After the fire he moved from New York City to Boston, where he lived for the next 10 years. Money, of course, was a problem: by one account he lived, in Thoreau fashion, like a mendicant.

Under contract to Seymour Lawrence, he continued producing regular work, publishing his second collection of stories, *Liars in Love,* and a novel, *Young Hearts Crying,* in the early 1980s. *Liars in Love* was compared to *Eleven Kinds of Loneliness,* not always favorably but not always fairly either. *Young Hearts Crying,* too, was perceived as deriving much of its virtue from Yates's earlier work, particularly *Disturbing the Peace*—the two plots are superficially alike, in that both protagonists become institutionalized, though a reasonable argument can be made that *Young Hearts Crying* is the stronger novel of the two, since it avoids the melodrama of *Disturbing the Peace's* final scene. Unlike *Disturbing the Peace,* which ends with John Wilder in the mental ward where he will doubtless be spending the rest of his life, *Young Hearts Crying* ends with Michael Davenport sadly but calmly and rationally assessing his life. Davenport's second marriage (to a much younger woman) is probably breaking apart, but he is clearly not going to break. He is shown, instead, trying to accept his own propensity for being alone. Yates's own second marriage, to a younger woman much like the second wife in *Young Hearts Crying,* lasted only a few years, ending in divorce in the mid-1970s. According to Yates's friend Geoffrey Clark, he was turned down for a job at Amherst College in 1976: Yates wrote that he went "through the sweaty business of reading & asskissing at Amhearst," only to be given "the coughdrop," the blackball of rejection. "The dept. chairman's letter was some lame nonsense to the effect that there is some agitation to hire a woman or a black."[15]

In 1981 he was offered a visiting professorship in the graduate creative writing program at Boston University. In *Young Hearts Crying* he describes Michael Davenport, a poet, getting "a letter . . . from the chairman of the English Department at Boston University, and it was a clear and definite offer of employment. The final sentence of it [read]. . . . 'Apart from the business at hand, let me say that I have always considered "Coming Clean" to be among the finest poems written in this country since the Second World War' " (*YHC,* 326).

Those sentiments were perfectly analogous to the Boston University program director's enthusiasm for *Eleven Kinds of Loneliness* when he hired Yates.[16] Yates's BU students, like his graduate students elsewhere, took to him warmly as well—they expressed their affection by coming to his apartment occasionally to clean it and, at least one time, to sand down his floors for him. But as he did almost everywhere he went, Yates soon moved on. In 1984 he took another brief position at Emerson College in Boston. None of the teaching positions he took after Iowa ever offered him even a chance of getting tenure, so his life continued its peripatetic path. Like F. Scott Fitzgerald, while he was growing up his family changed houses practically every year, and also like Fitzgerald, he chose to continue doing so for the rest of his life. "As long as I've lived," he said in 1989, "getting out of where I am has seemed an appealing idea" (Venant).

In 1986 he moved out to California again, where a former student, now a successful producer of television dramas, offered Yates work writing a TV pilot, which never aired, about a Washington, D.C., newspaper. In the late 1980s Yates moved into a Los Angeles apartment with his daughter, Monica, a nurse, and for the first extended period in his adult life, cut back severely on his use of tobacco and alcohol. When not employed as a scriptwriter, he took another nontenured teaching position, this time at the University of Southern California.

In 1990 he was offered a one-year visiting appointment to teach at the University of Alabama at Tuscaloosa, where he was able to occupy a home for visiting faculty, which his daughter described as a fancy one by Yates's standards.[17] His first apartment in Los Angeles, where he had been living against all odds without a car, had resembled a makeshift office more than a home (Venant). In the spring of 1991, with his visiting appointment over, he had found the cost of living in Tuscaloosa sufficiently low to permit him to live on his Social Security benefits, for which he had just become eligible (MY interview).

After publishing his last novel, *Cold Spring Harbor*, in 1986 to respectable reviews, Yates worked on a novel based on his experiences in Washington writing speeches for Robert Kennedy, tentatively entitled *Uncertain Times*. But his lungs, which had been bad for almost 50 years, by now were weakening, and he spent his last year able to write haltingly at best. Attached at times to an oxygen tank, he felt alert enough to write for only an hour or so a day, and he had always been the sort of slow, deliberate writer for whom an hour of work was often required to adjust the punctuation in one sentence.[18] He died of emphysema in the Veterans Administration hospital in Birmingham on 7 November 1992.

He had a "terrible honesty," Raymond Chandler's phrase for the kind of bluntness that tends to cost people their jobs, their friends, sometimes their happiness. In *Young Hearts Crying*, his protagonist, full of drink but not nearly drunk, defends an unpopular political position against his boss, the chairman of the English department where he works. This unseemly argument is all to defend a casual acquaintance whom he will probably never see again. It's hard to imagine Yates lacking the courage or the temperament to create such problems for himself. That episode, published in *Esquire* as a short story entitled "The Right Thing," exemplified Yates's strict stance against dishonesty, sloppy thinking, and trendy posturing. Raised in an era and a culture and a household that encouraged alcohol abuse, and which often defended it in the disguise of frank speaking, Yates tended to attract admirers and then inexorably drive them from him. As a teacher of creative writing, for example, Yates could be blunt, a trait that students alternatively adore and despise. DeWitt Henry, his student at Iowa and later his interviewer, editor, teaching colleague, and friend, found Yates a dedicated teacher who had "an instinctive and profound acuity when it came to seeing the heart of a story." Henry quoted another student who had written about Yates's relentless "hectoring about precision of language," stipulating that he took "hectoring" to be a virtue.[19] Another former student, Geoffrey Clark, noted that for a guy often thought to put more trust in intuition than ratiocination, "Dick was astonishingly logical on literary matters of all kinds, and was especially good at finding little hitches or illogicalities in a work, or something in an action sequence that was out of whack: those little but significant things so important to those of us trying to learn the craft" (Clark, 30).

When choosing short stories for the anthology *Stories for the Sixties,* he set his standards high, forcing himself to do much more work than most anthologists. Typically, editing such an anthology means poring over some recent anthologies, culling the best selections, and perhaps adding a few unheralded favorites. Instead, Yates actually read thousands of stories submitted by unknown writers. (The most successful of them turned out to be Judith Rossner, whose story bore a Yatesian title: "My True Story, If Anyone Cares.") Yates's praise for the stories he picked typified his standards for fiction: "None of them," he explained, "betrays the uncomfortable sound of an author trying to speak in a voice that is not his own."[20] Mere technical facility, in other words, didn't impress Yates nearly as much as writing that succeeded, above all else, in telling the truth as the author saw it.

The challenge Yates set for himself was to select details, out of the many he had witnessed, that made those truths unmistakable to his reader. Choosing those details, Yates felt, was his art. When someone praised Yates's ingenuity in structuring the ending of *The Easter Parade,* he denied inventing that scene. It took place, he explained, almost exactly as it did in the novel; the character's names were even the same, and so on. "But," he allowed, with a touch of pride in his voice, "I'm the one who saw it" (*RY*, 22). As with the protagonist of "The Right Thing," Yates's characters often lack the self-control that might temper their harshness and ease their lives. The title of that story implies that there are things that are right and, by further implication, things that are wrong, and Yates's assertion to that effect was at sharp odds with the relativistic view that obtained in his time. Yates turned his limitations into his subject matter, and accepted the reality of his limitations as a person (Yates would have proudly phrased that "as a man") and as a writer.

Chapter 3

Revolutionary Road and the Great Expectations of the 1950s

Published in 1961, *Revolutionary Road* was the brilliant opening of a problematic career. In many ways it delivered the best Yates was capable of as a realistic novelist: searingly vivid characters who emerge from the insipid 1950s setting; a vacuous and chilling suburban landscape that puts a fatalistic charge on every dramatic scene; a sentence-to-sentence style that registers every false hope and terrifying letdown of its people. Yates would exhibit some or most of these qualities in his other novels, but nowhere else do they come together so successfully.

The book won immediate critical recognition and left Yates with the obligations of a writer who had created a standard within the genre of the contemporary social novel. Without drawing attention to his skills through bravura passages, idea-soaked stretches of dialogue, or overly ingenious plotting, Yates succeeded where bigger talents, even Hemingway in the postwar period, had been running into the sands with melodrama, hokey dialogue and characters, and mannered prose. James Atlas, a judicious critic of contemporary American literature, didn't mind rhapsodizing when he pronounced the book "one of the few novels I know that could be called flawless."[1]

An early draft of the work, submitted to Atlantic–Little, Brown in 1956 after a year's work, did not elicit such praise. The response was that Yates had produced yet another version of *The Man in the Gray Flannel Suit;* the chapters were thereafter labored over until 1960. At one point the manuscript had the lackluster title *Contemporary Life on the Eastern Seaboard;* soon after, it was called *The Stragglers,* an obvious reference to Frank and April Wheeler's capacity to lag far behind their great plans. When the book finally emerged as *Revolutionary Road,* the executives at Little, Brown thought the title was too subtle. Yates evidently held his ground. He also removed the stereotypical qualities and slack writing that failed to impress his publisher, and that he himself admitted made the draft "superficial." The manuscript reached the publisher's office in need of "no editing and very little copyediting. It was perfectly made," according to Yates's editor and longtime friend Seymour Lawrence (*RY*, 56). And it has taken its place as one of the most highly crafted works of realistic fiction of its era. Its hold on critics and readers can be traced to a variety of formal qualities, powerful emotions, and enduring ideas.

Structure and Style

Yates's plot line has the elegant simplicity and tragic force of a classic play about a passion gone wrong. April and Frank Wheeler, a well-educated and attractive couple in post–World War II New York, set out to satisfy their vague but deep yearnings for personal authenticity, golden friends, and a life that can rise gracefully above their frustrating childhoods. They meet at a Morningside Heights party, spend a lyrical and dreamy period in Greenwich Village, and then go up to Connecticut in the early 1950s to settle in as parents of two small children. Their decision about moving to the suburbs is made almost on impulse, before they have clarified their own desires or come to grips with a strange discontent that is never quite specified.

In a small white house near Revolutionary Estates, a hideous, expensive new development, they settle into a routine of fighting and recriminating until they come up with a scheme about escaping to Europe. Sustained for months by guidebooks, endless talks about discovering their identities, and pathetic ideas about transcendence through sophistication, they are soon faced with April's pregnancy, Frank's new job prospects, and the apparent collapse of their plans. After the disappointment, Frank tries to rationalize their position, April sees him for the weak and complacent man he is, and both partners employ some of the more savage strategies of marital pitched battle: dredged-up accusations, silence, and digs about each other's mental instability and emptiness. All the while, even to the brink of April's abortion and death, the couple is surrounded by the throwaway culture of 1950s suburbia, the gaping "maw" of the TV, the tackiness of Route 12, the half-hearted and amateurish forays into culture of their neighbors, the prissy gentility of the local real estate agent.

Divided into three sections, the book presents the 1955 story of the Wheelers' downfall while using flashbacks and fade-outs to fill in their pasts. Part 1 starts in 1955 with an embarrassingly bad production by the Laurel Players, flashes back to the years after the war, and telescopes scenes from youth. It then moves forward into a world of falling expectations in Connecticut. A good part of the section is taken up with documenting the downside of weekends, days at Frank's office, visits from neighbors. Yates meticulously builds a mood of desperation: as the Wheelers socialize with the dull Campbells and start to get sick of each other's poses and mannerisms, the tension rises. Just as they reach their breaking point, April leads her husband into an improbable drama of life elsewhere. She proposes an escape from the "soap opera" of bourgeois family life. As they make love and manufacture fantasies about the bohemian life on the continent, the section ends.

Part 2 is as hollowly buoyant as part 1 has been genuinely bleak. "There now began a time of such joyous derangement, of such exultant carelessness that Frank Wheeler could never remember how long it lasted" (*RR,* 119). Everything that had a negative charge in part 1— evenings at home, conversations with the Campbells, even Frank's job—brightens up. Frank, whose discourses on conformity and Senator Joseph McCarthy were getting stale, again becomes the charmer that April once fell for. The woman who had just recently been nauseated by his rhetoric in part 1 is enraptured and anxious to hear more about "what's killing the United States," as it happens, those old chestnuts the bomb and cultural barrenness (*RR,* 128).

The chapters of part 2 build up false expectations about what talking, dreaming, and mutual understanding can accomplish. Yates uses a plot technique reminiscent of Flaubert's counterpointing in *Madame Bovary:* minor characters and incidents reinforce the meaning and irony of the main action. Yates devotes his chapters to other people who live in a cloud of vague yearnings. Shep Campbell, a neighbor who once revolted against his exclusive Manhattan background by trying to be a tough (and subsequently trying to be a highbrow), now dreams of making love to April; Mrs. Givings, the tony realtor, invents a world where her demented son John converses with the attractive Wheelers in a *Better Homes and Gardens* colonial setting; John himself talks nonsensical sense about American failure and emptiness. In his Manhattan office cubicle Frank hears more pretentious nonsense from Jack Ordway, a glamorous drunk and do-nothing who has Fitzgeraldian tales to tell about weekend parties with his broken-down socialite wife. The main thread of this section, the Wheelers' period of ardor and hope, is strengthened by Yates's command of many different kinds of yearning: even Maureen Grube, the secretary Frank carries on with, daydreams about her roommate's interesting friends and sophisticated tastes.

Part 2, a brilliantly arranged house of cards, collapses when April gets pregnant and Frank, for the first time in his life, gets drawn into his career. When Frank does a few good days' work on a promotional brochure, his small success brings on a major crisis: the Wheelers must face the fact that a good job and another child seem to be closing in on them. This time Frank concocts his own soap opera in which he is the kindly, responsible, mature leading man who all the while admires himself in the mirror. In despair with the pretense of it all, April threatens to abort their child.

Part 3 concerns time running out: it begins with an ironic reflection on comforting markers, dates we like to remember, and moves with ruthless efficiency through the deadlines in the characters' lives: April's planned date for aborting the child and spiting complacent Frank; Frank's relief when the date comes and goes; other appointments for the supporting characters, including John Givings's last visit with the Wheelers (and last day out of the state mental hospital), Maureen Grube's last rendezvous with Frank (an absurd disaster); Shep's one and only chance to make love to April.

The summer of 1955 is almost over as this section begins. Yates takes us into the catastrophe of early fall and then concludes by moving ahead to early spring 1956. Shep is reminded of the hopes of the Laurel Players; Mrs. Givings, the rather hardened survivor, is looking forward to the new people who have taken the Wheelers' house. Shep objects to his wife's soap opera style in her recounting of the Wheelers' ruin. Mrs. Givings can only recall their weird behavior and the fact that they neglected the nice sedum planting she collected for them. Mr. Givings turns off his hearing aid while his wife is talking.

Yates's craftsmanship is evident throughout: using the conventions of the well-made play, he builds the conflict to the point where Frank brutally refers to April's desire for an abortion, "I wish to God you'd done it" (*RR*, 291). This of course reveals his false decency. In preparation for this, Yates has stripped away many other illusions. Even a cracked, discredited character like John Givings can see through Frank's double talk. The sloppy pretending of the Wheelers jumps off the page. And Shep's romantic desire for April is so much lust. In the wrong hands this material would be no more than pathetic episodes from botched lives. Yates the craftsman brings vision, style, and characterization that make the reader wonder about the mysterious reaches of contemporary unhappiness and ask questions about what is genuine in our society.[2] He lifts his subject matter above merely deterministic stories about failure.

Yates's primary resource, his sentence style, is a supple instrument for bringing people and scenes into focus. Often clipped in phrasing like

Hemingway, he is also capable of writing Fitzgeraldian passages that reproduce the ardors of his characters. Frank Wheeler comes across as a mix of the sententious and the poetic, a man who is at once not to be believed and all too moving in his perceptions: "his mind went back to the first few years after the war and to a crumbling block of Bethune Street, in that part of New York where the gentle western edge of the Village flakes off into silent waterfront warehouses, where the salt breeze of evening and the deep river horns of night enrich the air with a promise of voyages" (*RR*, 20). Combining the austere with the lyrical, Yates manages to capture the essences of characters and places without crushing them under the weight of irony or smothering them with emotion. Such a style allows us to see through Frank Wheeler without getting tired of him: as Yates extends and withdraws sympathy—making Wheeler at times a young man of considerable charm and insight, at other times a pompous fool—he achieves the poise of a creator in command.

A line like the following exhibits a kind of wit and affection reminiscent of Fitzgerald on Jay Gatsby: "As an intense, nicotine-stained, Jean-Paul Sartre sort of man, wasn't it simple logic to expect that he'd be limited to intense, nicotine-stained, Jean-Paul Sartre sorts of women?" (*RR*, 23). Elsewhere Frank is allowed to breathe as a character because, even at his worst, he is given his measure of liveliness and intelligence. His diatribes are often witty, and certainly the best commentary that comes out of anyone's mouth. This, for example: "A man could rant and smash and grapple with the State Police, and still the sprinklers whirled at dusk on every lawn and the television droned in every room" (*RR*, 65).

April is given all a novelist can give such a victim: words that are not flat, descriptions of her character that make her problems mysterious rather than merely clinical. When Shep Campbell refuses to believe that April, his ideal of glamour and loveliness, could ever have been lonely, she responds in lines that raise her above the level of the furious, vengeful partner of Frank: "Bless you, Shep. I always hoped people wouldn't picture me being that lonely. That was really the best thing about being in New York after the war, you see. People didn't" (*RR*, 257).

Yates's style also mirrors the social confusion of suburbia without thundering or lecturing like Frank. Blending pity and irony, Yates coordinates the landscape with the fragmented lives of the characters. A bleak winter afternoon makes the houses look "as foolishly misplaced as a great many bright new toys left out overnight and rained on" (*RR*, 5). In the same scene candy-colored cars "crawled apologetically" along broken back roads until they reached the tacky plastic and stainless steel of Route 12. Like the apologetic cars, the people in the book don't feel quite right about their environment most of the time; and even when they reach a stretch of experience that seems to match their qualities— an ordinary troubled marriage, a compromising job—they can't feel easy for long. Yates's style, in all its deceptive plainness, rarely allows the reader to settle into the satisfactions of satire, savage irony, or melodrama. He constantly modulates his language and forces his audience to respond to a variety of emotions at once.

Characters: The Disaffected and the Distraught

The material of *Revolutionary Road* is hardly unique: a collection of neurotics posed against a suburban backdrop is the stock in trade of the pop sociologist, the songwriter, and the typical author of the fictional exposé. Writing about conformity is in itself a conventional occupation. But Yates uses his wit and his grasp of the bourgeois idiom of whining and complaint to reach a higher level of understanding about what's wrong in America. His characters are depicted as baffled despite their knowingness: their talk of Freud is either flippant and dismissive (an attitude to be found throughout Yates's work) or literal minded and simplistic. Frank, for example, mocks the headshrinkers, but doesn't mind lecturing his wife on penis envy. The horror of suburban "togetherness" is another favorite topic of complaint: Yates has Frank saying, in a phrase reminiscent of D. H. Lawrence, that American suburban children are brought up "in a bath of sentimentality" (*RR*, 66). Of course the problem here is that pat analysis of society often reads like a bad joke played on the characters themselves. The Wheelers' children—two bewildered specks of humanity—haven't even evolved to the point where they are especially sentimental about anything.

The cast of ineffectual characters includes people of every level of awareness and intelligence. Although Yates draws attention to the smarter and more sensitive characters, he also wants us to see the yawning gaps in their logic and perceptions. While he creates a few minor characters who hardly seem to know what's going on, he insists that we watch their perceptions as well. Insight in *Revolutionary Road,* as in *Madame Bovary,* is found in the crevices of every chapter, not in grand speeches; it's often possible for a foolish character, say, Mrs. Givings, to stumble on a truth. Skeptical, ironic, and sly, Yates avoids the predictable solution of having a reliable central character lead us through confusing territory.

Frank Wheeler's dialogue, daydreaming, and actions—as well as Yates's authorial comments—are carefully structured to carry through the novel's central ideas of confusion, status yearning, and ineptitude. Although Frank's youthful ambitions are quite vague, it is clear enough that he wants to be an authentic self and a memorable character. In his teenage years he fantasized about hopping a freight train going West (in Levi jacket and old felt hat, of course) and discovering his destiny. When a friend called him a jerk, he awakened to the theme of his life: that you're never a jerk if you're pursuing a lyrical dream.

Frank embodies the spirit of an age in the way Jay Gatsby once did. Gatsby invented himself by name dropping, scheming, and manipulating powerful and glamorous people; Frank Wheeler built his identity on post–World War II style. Jay Gatsby lived off his gangster-gentleman mystique; Frank lived off the late 1940s image of the knockabout intellectual—cool, not class-conscious, uncommitted to the rewards of the society. For all his illusions, Gatsby had the clarity of mind to write down his Ben Franklin–like rules for getting ahead in life; James J. Hill and the bully boys of the late nineteenth century were his models. By contrast, Frank turned to vague bits of existentialism—notably ideas about the nauseating quality of life, the liberation to be found in risk, and the essential absurdity of living.

While Gatsby tried to win Daisy with romantic blandishments, Frank courted April with the world-weary line of the pre-Beat generation intellectual at odds with Pax Americana; he got the girl by being an amateur social critic, sounding at times like the young Norman Mailer who told *Partisan Review* symposium members in 1952, "This period smacks of healthy manifestoes. Everywhere the American writer is being dunned to become healthy, to grow up, to accept the American reality, to integrate himself, to eschew disease, to re-value institutions."[3] When Frank first met April, she wanted to know what he was "really interested in" (*RR*, 24). Too aware of the absurd to be earnest, too put off by conventions to talk about a career, Frank answered, "Honey, if I had the answer to that one I bet I'd bore us both to death in half an hour" (*RR*, 24).

There is of course a certain magnetism to all this: disaffection with American progress and plenty fueled the literary culture of the 1960s, lit a fire under torpid institutions, and dislodged the nation from its complacencies about race, international relations, and the beneficence of American ideals. The trouble with Frank, however, is that his disaffection leads neither to writing, nor action, nor creative ways of turning life around. He remains an unconventional man who is too cool to be involved with American life and too sheepish to live against the grain. This type—for it is, after all, a type—can be clumsily handled, used as a mere straw man to be discredited by well-adjusted people. Herman Wouk's Noel Airman in *Marjorie Morningstar* (1955) is an inferior version of Wheeler: too individual to accommodate himself to commercialism, never good enough to leave his role as big man in a Catskill resort theater; too interesting to fit the mold of business, yet not interesting enough to be an artist. Ultimately, as the critic Isaac Rosenfeld has so wittily pointed out, Airman is an inferior version of the nowhere dreamer, the *Luftmensch* of Jewish lore: "the psychoanalytic double talk, the cuteness, narcissism and lint of Village beds, which stigmata are meant to stand in indictment of the man, and the sophomoric philosophizing, intended to take care of his intellectual pretensions" make the character into a reductive, unconvincing mess.[4]

Airman, at times almost the cartoon seducer of nice Jewish girls, is right out of the cliché warehouse. But Frank, for all his talkiness, is very credible; the saddest thing about his life is that he is dead right about suburban denial, TV sentimentality, decadence. His yearnings and restlessness are not without sense and make him more complex than Noel Airman, the Jewish mother's nightmare. His tragedy is that he uses his fairly superior gifts for nothing higher than cocktail conversation and brochure writing. He imagines that some great thing will take hold of his life if he can only keep faith with his principles.

April is at once the victim of Frank's charm and the destroyer of what little vitality he possesses. Like some Madame Bovary transplanted to the 1950s (at one point Frank even mocks her for playing the part of Flaubert's character), she yearns for glamour, the love of a masterful and imaginative man, and the promise of escape from domestic routine. Yates specifically referred to the influence of Flaubert in a *New York Times Book Review* article: *Madame Bovary* was the "guide" for the novel "taking shape in my mind"; it offered, among other things, a "kind of inexorable destiny in the heart of a lonely, romantic girl" ("Masters," 3).

April, like Emma, is trapped in her bourgeois setting, married to a man who enrages her with his smugness, and furiously in pursuit of an escape route. Restless and frenetic while her husband is inert, she seems to undergo the same torture that Emma goes through as she listens to Charles Bovary drone on. But Frank, of course, is a good deal livelier than poor Charles: while he is also headed nowhere, he moves there with a certain style and superficial command. And almost like Emma's lovers,

Frank has teased April with glimmering prospects without delivering anything more than sex and talk. Like Flaubert, Yates explores the nature of the disappointment by showing the nonsense that a woman must accept simply because her man has nothing better to offer. Flaubert's Rodolphe Boulanger showers Emma with cheap fantasies, including an imaginative flight in which their dead mothers look down on the happy lovers. April receives similar overwrought speeches about Frank's intense feelings. "He felt tense and keyed up; the very act of sitting on a coffee table seemed an original and wonderful thing to do" (RR, 129). In this dizzy state he compares their awakening to "coming out of a Cellophane bag" (RR, 129), and soon after he adds that it's like his exhilarating experience of going into combat in the army. April, like Emma, thrives on such stuff and comments that she has felt the same way: "The first time you made love to me" (RR, 130). At certain points of soap operatic oneness (rendered, of course, ironically), it becomes difficult for the reader to sort out the origins of the couple's illusions; "their embraces of the eye," Yates tells us, are very conscious bits of showmanship. But who is the more arresting performer?

For all his living room philosophizing, Frank lacks April's disturbing energy. Yates follows her through a year of chilling performances, outbursts to stage her own mysterious needs. On the Laurel Players' stage or in the living room, she exhibits a curious blend of intensity and theatrical ineptitude. A director would probably see that she wants the role but doesn't quite understand the significance of the drama. When she is talking with Frank her voice has "a quality of playacting, of slightly false intensity, a way of seeming to speak less to him than to some romantic abstraction." During the year she lurches from one badly played part to the next: the Laurel Players' production of *The Petrified Forest* features April in the part of Gabrielle, a young girl marooned in a desolate service restaurant out west who wants to go to Europe and "do something that's absolutely crazy, and marvelous" (RR, 8). Meanwhile, her role involves her with a discoursing intellectual Englishman who charms her with his *weltschmerz*, his little-boy vulnerability, and his smooth romantic line. Playing the part of Gabrielle, essentially acting a melodramatic equivalent of her real-life role, is April's first disaster in *Revolutionary Road*.

At the curtain call April's face is "paralyzed in a formal smile" (RR, 10). Soon after she plays her next part with Frank: the devastated wife, raging because he wants to talk, rationalize her failure, and inject himself into her world of pain and disappointment. She stages a knock-down-drag-out quarrel, complete with a screaming scene on the side of a high-way. For an entire weekend she plays the injured party, making Frank seem like the source of her bad acting. By Monday evening, it's on to another part: the romantic adventuress on the brink of a new life abroad. This storm-calm motif—hysteria followed by eerie contentment—foreshadows the final sections of the novel. In these terrifying pages April moves from her scene of towering rage and vituperation, complete with her mad escape into the dark wood behind their property, to the chilling calm of the breakfast scene the next morning with Frank. This scene shows April in all her scary serenity, being the good wife sending her husband off to work before performing an abortion on herself.

The pathos of her situation is contained in the idea of acting itself: for years she has had to pretend to believe in a weak man's rationalizations, in an empty community's pleasures, and in a diminishing number of good parts for herself. Yates never lets us forget April's desperate attempts to manage and perform: crucial passages show her arranging decor, dress, and dialogue in an attempt to project a mood. But the only role that seems convincingly worked out in every scene in which she appears is that of the woman poised for flight. Yates uses this image to convey the disorder of her life and to fascinate a reader who might otherwise be merely sickened by April's neurosis.

Frank and April are about as narcissistic, idle, and loveless a pair as one is likely to find in contemporary American literature. Poses take up almost all the time that other fictional characters use for work and love-making. By the standards of his time, Yates is singularly unconcerned with exhilarating success stories or juicy sex scenes. The motor of his narrative seems to be turned over by the power of dueling egos: the Wheelers' dialogue cuts and slashes, leaving us with the emptiest sounds of its era. While playing psychoanalyst, Frank accuses April of denying her femininity: as he reads it, she has wanted to terminate all three of her pregnancies. For a moment the reader finds a certain plausibility in his remark, if only because it fits the facts of her destructive nature. Yet his argument collapses when he accuses her of insanity—by his own definition, the inability to love. Coming from a lecher and a hot-air artist, this pronouncement rings hollow. And poor April's problem is that she has come unprepared into a world where the socially and psychologically fragile get little understanding. Mostly they get speeches, formulas, and cant of various sorts.

Frank and April are bound together by a web of false words that sound like nothing so much as a description of the hollowness of contemporary rhetoric offered by the cultural critic Harold Rosenberg. "Individualism," "identity," "finding yourself" are the words that have taken over the Wheelers' lives. Rosenberg describes such people—hardly the masses or the uninstructed—as a "herd of independent minds," a segment of the middle class in the grip of "common experience" rather than "the experience of being."[5] Sour bohemians, come-lately expatriates, dabblers in the arts and ideas have never engaged in what Rosenberg calls "the single human being's effort to arrive at a consciousness of himself" (Rosenberg, 21). Frank and April, the nicotine-stained Jean-Paul Sartre man and the actress poised for flight, seem to do little more than rake over the vocabulary of complaint.

Yates uses several minor characters to reinforce the effect of the Wheelers' story. Continuing his theatrical motif, he shows the absurd ways in which these people manage impressions of themselves. Sometimes they provide comic relief in a book that is ruthless in its pursuit of illusions. Foremost among them is John Givings, the mentally disturbed truth teller. Living out at Greenacres, the state hospital, he has rebelled against his obnoxiously controlling and genteel mother and his inert father (the castrating Mommy and the ineffectual Daddy that Frank Wheeler has seen as the prototypical TV characters) by going mad without the good grace of the nice middle-class disturbed person. Refusing to wear his tweed jacket and cashmere sweater, John prefers to dress like an institutionalized person and violate all the proprieties of Revolutionary Road. He asks blunt questions, drinks sherry out of a tumbler, and refuses to see the rainbows that his mother points to. His visits to the Wheelers with his parents are a collection of embarrassing and sometimes hilarious moments designed to shake up the squares and bring on recognitions about the emptiness-of-it-all.

The by now very familiar figure of the intelligent mental patient, the questioner of conventions who is branded as a nut case, is handled with great skill. For all his sardonic wit, John is made into a rather repellent figure, hardly the delight maker or folk hero of romantic fiction. Yates the realist establishes a just proportion for the character, refusing to make him endearing or brave. Ken Kesey's romanticism in *One Flew Over the Cuckoo's Nest* is far from Yates's chilling appraisals of what crazy people are likely to do. While John forces April and Frank to see their inability to act, he is rude and cruel and destructive. While he gloats over his mother's transparent denials and evasions—including her tendency to rhapsodize about the tastiness of April's egg salad—he becomes a critic of weak people, as well as a part of the destructive chain of relations in the novel.

His mother, Helen, is more complexly rendered, even though she is far less intelligent than he and is a far more familiar bourgeois type. Boring and petty people come alive when Yates moves through their routines; with Flaubertian precision, he follows their gaffes and nails down their traits by specifying every absurd action and opinion. Yates himself drew attention to this strategy by pointing out a passage in Flaubert that meant a great deal to him: the scene in *Madame Bovary* in which Charles relishes a basket of apricots—"Smell that fragrance!"—is the same scene in which Emma has just taken her lover's farewell letter from the top of the basket ("Masters," 3).

Yates's debt to the French master anatomist of mediocrity can be seen in the portrait of Mrs. Givings. Like Homais, the apothecary in *Madame Bovary,* she is a sententious authority on the good life and the finer points of domesticity. The 1950s equivalent of Flaubert's smug, nosy neighbor, she busies herself with feeling superior, observing vulgarity in the neighborhood, and evaluating the social credentials of newcomers. Her world of smarmy niceness, like Homais's vulgar optimism, is subjected to close scrutiny; the omniscient point of view, used sparingly on April Wheeler, is turned up high for a look at this ludicrous woman. In one sense she is a victim of petit bourgeois ideas of respectability overlaid with tony notions of taste and gracious living. Her evaluations of people are most often catty: of John's psychiatrist she wonders how you could feel "anything but soiled in the presence of a red-eyed, nail-biting little man who used adhesive tape to hold his glasses together and a piece of Woolworth jewelry to keep his tie clamped flat against his white-on-white shirt" (*RR,* 153). (Paul Fussell, the author of *Class,* employs many of the same class indicators as Yates.) She sells houses to "impossibly rude people whose children ran tricycles against her shins and spilled Kool-Aid on her dress" (*RR,* 153). She thinks of her home with its wineglass elms as a "final bastion against vulgarity" (*RR,* 152).

Such a combination of snobbery and bitchiness is strangely effective in producing an all-too-human character. Who wouldn't prefer the pre-Revolutionary home with its smell of cedar and beeswax to the tackiness of the ranch houses and the custard stands of Route 12? Mrs. Givings is also essentially a sad figure who finds comfort in a small piece of a classier American dream—not a two-car garage, but some oak paneling and a grandfather clock. She goes no deeper than these small desires, but Yates makes her meager, tidy world memorable because it is set against a landscape of chaos. She also seems closed off from any larger, more generous conception of happiness. There is reason enough here for her son's mental troubles, or so Yates would have us believe. And yet the way her life has been designed seems to leave room for little more than middle-class survival and self-protection. Like many of Yates's other characters, she doesn't have the emotional repertoire to take in the otherness of those around her. She labels people and can barely read any indicator of identity that does not relate to class. Her best skills, steadiness and basic civility, put her at a loss when she is faced with the sloppiness of intense suffering.

The other minor characters also muddle through their routines without showing much ability to grow or understand the fragments of their lives. Shep Campbell, the Wheeler's neighbor, is accorded the same authorial treatment as Mrs. Givings: Yates's alternation between sympathy and distance, between omniscient understanding of Shep's past and cold presentation of his present. This switching makes Shep, despite his stolid stupidity, a well-realized person. While Mrs. Givings is seen prospering in her real estate deals and enjoying her antique coffee table, Shep is presented as an American who has lost ground in the race for status and gracious living. Mrs. Givings, the pathetic striver, has moved up in the social scale; Shep, the kid raised on Sutton Place who rebelled against his background, has moved downward. Since Shep's story is told from the inside by a narrator who assumes his character's attitudes, we can't assume any snobbery on the part of the narrator; and yet the downward slide of the character is rather brutally and condescendingly depicted. Shep first slides to the level of an engineering student at a faceless Midwestern university, then to a barren existence at an Arizona hydraulics plant, and finally to Revolutionary Road's sterility. Here his living room has a roaring TV, his wife has a line of inane patter, and his job at Allied Precision has no character whatsoever.

In portraying Shep, Yates demonstrates his superb grasp of the American class structure. Not quite satiric, yet clearly critical, Yates's rendering of uppers, middles, and lower-middles makes the reader think that the authorial voice is taking stock of every weakness in every location. While F. Scott Fitzgerald privileged Nick Carraway and old money, Yates seems to deride everyone: the author who suffered the hidden injuries of class seems to harp on the vulnerabilities and judge the victims of class consciousness harshly. Shep's mother—dressing her little boy in kilts from Bergdorf Goodman, tearfully pleading with the young tough to go to Princeton—is as ridiculous as Mrs. Givings. The dynamic here is found everywhere in Yates's work: a high-toned, pretentious mother tries to make her son a young gentleman; the young man, whether Shep or Bob Prentice in *A Special Providence,* is surly and sometimes cultivates the manner of the lout. What this all adds up to is a rather pessimistic, not to say puzzling, account of what it's like to be caught in the American class system: whether you look upward or downward the prospects are fairly gruesome. And you're going to be warped wherever you are.

When Shep is stuck with his wife and new baby in Arizona, Yates spares the middle class nothing: the description of their situation includes "a sun-baked box of a house with four framed mountain scenes from the dimestore," five brown engineering manuals in the bookshelves, the aforementioned booming TV, and the "shrill noise of the neighbors dropping in for Canasta" (*RR,* 138). For a time Shep goes crazy, which is to say, Yates has him revolting and becoming a bohemian and reader of literary journals who cultivates a British accent. Yet the protest against American tackiness, handled with style by Frank Wheeler, is in this case merely pathetic: when Shep comes east to the land of the Ivy League and culture, he merely submits to a Connecticut version of his dismal existence. The high point of his life is making love in the back of a car to classy April: this rather sordid scene doesn't even cause Shep to wake up to the truth of his own warped life. The oaf who has just seduced a severely depressed woman soon will be asking when he can see her again.

Shep's main problem is similar to the Wheelers' malaise: he has spent his life playing parts in which he has miscast himself. The language of the theater is embedded in the stretches of description that concern him: he "saved" his peasant/tough guy expression for certain occasions; he was uneasy with "the high adventure of pretending to be something that he was not"; he even allowed himself, after April's death, to be "cued" by his wife when they told the neighbors about the Wheelers' tragedy (*RR,* 139).

There are other faulty performers in the novel, some of them comic fakers from Frank's office. And as is not usual in realistic fiction, the book's tragic figure comes from the pack of jokers. Relieving the tensions of the narrative on several occasions, Yates lets us see that fakery can be laughable. As Frank avoids work, inspects the finer points of typists' figures, and plays the game of seeming busy, he comes off as a comic sketch. His desk is filled with undone work and unanswered memos—"Real Goodies" as he calls such items. His lunch hour is a struggle to get his colleagues to go to the Nice place (where drinks are available) rather than the Awful place (where you can smell the maple syrup and butter). His office friends include the poseur Jack Ordway, a brilliantly rendered drunk who puts on airs and owns one suit from a London tailor, and his mistress, Maureen Grube, a typist who yearns for the better things, including an artsy Greenwich Village lifestyle. Maureen lives in an apartment filled with Picasso prints, Book-of-the-Month Club selections, and other clumsy indicators of sophistication. Her manner is totally dopey, overeager, and out of keeping with Frank's coolness. Their last evening together is a comic debacle in which she tries to get him into bed while he tries to tell her that their affair is over. True to his vision of ineptitude and loss, Yates makes it come right before the Wheeler's downfall. He always has the strength of purpose and the honesty to let us see the absurdities and laughable mishaps in close proximity to the catastrophes.

The people in *Revolutionary Road* are all, in their own ways, like the sloppy members of the Steve Kovick Quartet, a group that gives its embarrassingly bad performances, paralleling the Laurel Players, at Vito's Log Cabin. The group had "no idea of what inferior musicians they were" (*RR*, 246). Their leader and drummer Steve thought of himself as professional "without ever quite learning his craft" (*RR*, 246). And without the equipment—the grace, taste, sense of timing, basic skills—Yates's characters continue to play their parts. On the brink of suicide, April thinks of the quartet and of herself; both are "earnest and sloppy and full of pretension and all wrong" (*RR*, 304). Even Mrs. Givings, who seems to be efficient and somewhat successful, is tirelessly attempting to cover up the truths of her life: she keeps busy, in her officious and sad way, in order to forget her own empty youth and her son's insanity. Caught up in managing impressions of themselves, these characters lose their identities.

Gruesome Toyland

Yates's limited people are further beaten down by dispiriting American locales. Like his characters, his places are uncomfortable and out of joint with human needs. A more unaccommodating landscape than Revolutionary Road would be hard to conceive. People clash horribly with the manufactured Arcadia—all pastels and greenery and floodlights. Several mordant scenes bring Yates's vision into focus: they seem to coordinate perfectly with frustration and hopelessness. The Wheelers' house has an outsized picture window "staring like a big black mirror" (*RR*, 29). The ominous image is followed by a substantial paragraph in which Frank and April rationalize about "the prim suburban look" of the interior:

maybe the "gathering disorder of their lives" can be made to fit the conventional symmetry of a post–World War II house (*RR,* 30). But in a scene that soon follows, we see Frank mindlessly spending a Saturday afternoon trying to build a stone path from his door to the road. The backbreaking, spirit-wasting work is given an added measure of pain by Frank's mood (it's the day after a fearsome quarrel with April) and by his children's nerve-racking questions and proximity to his shovel blade. The business of the day, like that of some suburban Sisyphus, is to deal with a boulder that he can't dislodge. The path, as we find, is never completed. A final image of desolation appears in the scene in which Frank, maddened with grief after his wife's death, tries to cut across Revolutionary Estates on foot to reach his property. The area, "an invincibly cheerful" toyland, makes him seem "indecently out of place" (*RR,* 323). TV applause emanates from the houses, lights play on the lawns, and the agonized man falls and grabs hold of a child's beach bucket.

The grimness of Yates's suburbia has been captured in James Howard Kunstler's *The Geography of Nowhere,* a social study of what Americans have done to their communities in the postwar period. Born in 1947, Kunstler grew up in a place that was trying to forget tradition, urban life, and the larger world: his Long Island suburban community seems as stranded as Revolutionary Road. His generalizations about the "American Dream of a cottage on its own sacred plot of earth" belong next to Yates's gruesome toyland:

> By the time the merchant builders like Levitt and his kindred spirits got through packaging it [the dream], however, it was less a dream than a cruel parody. The place where the dream house stood—a subdivision of many other dream houses—was neither the country nor the city. It was noplace. If anything, it combined the worst social elements of the city and the country and none of the best elements. As in the real country, everything was spread out and hard to get to without a car. There were no cultural institutions. And yet like the city, the suburb afforded no escape from other people into nature; except for some totemic trees and shrubs, nature had been obliterated by the relentless blocks full of houses (Kunstler, 105).

The condition of being neither wilderness nor orderly town, neither healing private retreat nor bustling public realm, neither solitude nor society, is Kunstler's master theme. Yates's unfocused lives and incoherent places also invite comparisons with the social commentator's purposes. (On the level of the simplest notation, poor Millie Campbell even

knows that she's not in the "real" country.) Kunstler is clear enough in
locating the blame for the trashing of America: our perverted optimism,
blind faith in the automobile, greed, and political irresponsibility have
landed us in the middle of nowhere at the end of the twentieth century.
What *Revolutionary Road* means is more difficult to answer. Did the
Wheelers get an atmosphere that they deserved, indeed, that their attitudes helped to create? Or were they mere victims of titanic market
forces that brought this world into being?

A Critique of Illusions

Although Yates is not a writer of "problem" novels—tendentious explo-
rations of everything from business skullduggery to race hatred—he
brings an acute intelligence to bear on the subtle problem of middle-
class unhappiness. The Wheelers carry the frustrated hopes of their generation. A *Partisan Review* symposium published in 1952, "Our Country
and Our Culture," examined the question of renewed faith in the American Dream: the participants generally argued that educated Americans
were ready to take a fresh look at the promise of our national life, and to
forget the resentments of the 1930s. But several of the respondents,
including Norman Mailer and the literary critic Leslie Fiedler, took issue
with the mood of optimism among their fellow intellectuals. Fiedler did
not see a new beginning at all, arguing instead that it was our faulty
confidence, so different from postwar European cynicism, that left us
wide open to tragedy: "Precisely the uncompromising optimism of
Americans makes every inevitable failure to accomplish what can only
be dreamed an unredeemable torment" ("Country" 1:296). Such hope,
of course, is April Wheeler's vague yearning for the golden people and
Frank's ungrounded, amorphous ideas about a good civilization. These
two innocents are the victims of their own ideas of entitlement.

    Fiedler says that writers have an obligation to explore the tragedy of
such lives. Yates's novel, it would seem, is the critic's dream come true.
The Wheelers' self-deceptions are not accidental or easily curable: neither pure fatalism nor reformism is at the core of Yates's book. Like
Fiedler, Yates seems to believe in "the irreducible residuum of human
weakness, sloth, self-love, and fear" (*RR*, 297). In many ways Yates is
the kind of writer Fiedler calls for: someone who refuses to deny the
"irreducible" weaknesses of a complacent era. "If he can resist the vulgar
temptation to turn a quick profit by making yet one more bestselling
parody of hope, and the snobbish temptation to burnish chic versions of

elegant despair, the American writer will find that he has, after all, a real function" ("Country" 1:298). Yates shows that the Wheelers, Campbells, and Givingses are implicated in the crime of despoiling the culture and the landscape. Their sufferings and protests do not diminish the force of their complacencies.

Although striking chords like those of Kunstler in our own time, as well as Fiedler and other critics in the 1950s, Yates takes the fiction writer's path: his evaluation of American faults does not indict General Motors or local government, but instead provides clear examples of how individuals passively let commerce and the neighbors swallow up their lives. The tone of *Revolutionary Road* also resembles Norman Mailer's contribution to "Our Country and Our Culture": almost like Frank Wheeler at his most convincing, Mailer thunders about the oppressive voice of society that has "dunned" writers and thinkers "to grow, be healthy, accept reality" ("Country," 1:299). But Yates's narrative voice pulls back from the declamatory style, leaving the speeches to his characters and to critics of the era.

Yates's book raises issues that can be found in thinkers whose ideas are much less sweeping and flamboyant than Fiedler's and Mailer's. As we have noted in chapter 1, Lionel Trilling's *The Liberal Imagination* sheds light on the intellectual shallowness of Yates's people: Trilling's description of liberalism gone stale—reduced to formulas about Freedom and Reality, deprived of its "variousness and possibility" by ideologues who prefer ideals and rallying cries to ideas—is very much like the denial of possibility and complexity to be found in the Wheelers' 1955 clichés about the American scene. According to Trilling, such people need to be returned to liberalism's first impulses: imagination and the recognition of complexity and difficulty.

In the same line of critical inquiry, Reinhold Niebuhr, a theologian and cultural critic of the 1950s, has identified another character weakness that can be found in *Revolutionary Road*. His small study *The Irony of American History* highlights what he believes to be an ironic national character flaw: the tendency to imagine that ideals liberate Americans from limitations. The "pretentious denial of human limits" is really a form of moral and intellectual blindness, an inability to perceive the complexity of experience.[6] The speechmaking and posturing of the Wheelers is a matter of high but confused ideals: they expect so much, but have calculated so few consequences. "Europe" and "civilization" are two of their ideals: suffice it to say that they have failed to consider either the limits of a ravaged Old World or the possibilities of their own

society. Thirty years too late for the Lost Generation, these would-be
expatriates are looking for renewal and rebirth not in Manhattan or
Chicago, the contemporary capitals of abstract expressionism and exper-
imentalism in literature and ideas, but in hungover Paris and Rome.
Yates supplies a "disquieting" moment of truth by making Frank think
of his own limits: more than likely April would be coming home from
her day at the office in some continental city and "finding him hunched
in an egg-stained bathrobe, on an unmade bed, picking his nose" (*RR*,
109). But by the next morning this recognition has vanished and Frank
is once again in the limitless and exhilarating territory of fantasy, where
"all sights are blurred and every task is easy" (*RR*, 120).

Critical Responses

Revolutionary Road was immediately recognized as a work of power and
high artistry. Its reviewers almost universally praised Yates's ability to
bring his essentially grim story to life. The objections raised—sometimes incisive and searching, sometimes obtuse—have more to do with
Yates's vision than his fictional technique. Orville Prescott in the *New
York Times* praised Yates's narrative skill but found the Wheelers to be
psychotic and therefore of little interest. An astonishing misreading of
character and cultural background can be seen in the following pronouncement: "Frank is not a recognizable type (he is too far gone in his
private fog of unreason) and 'Revolutionary Road' is only satirical in
passing."[7] Finally he adds, "Whether the mentally ill Wheelers deserve
the five years of labor Mr. Yates has lavished upon them is another question." A similar note is struck by the *Atlantic Monthly* reviewer who
objects to Yates's having made crazy John Givings a courageous mouthpiece for ideas about American hopelessness and desolation.[8]

Why are we paying so much attention to the negativism of these
casebook types? In the instance of the Prescott charge one can only
point out that Frank is an all-too-familiar neurotic who stumbles
through life, charms and damages those around him, but certainly has
no psychotic episodes. In the end, he's well accepted at the Knox Company and, in his glib and mechanical way, is a functional member of a
society that rewards millions like him. In later works Yates would portray characters over the edge, most notably John Wilder in *Disturbing
the Peace*. But here even April is merely a flighty and directionless
woman who has been cornered by life: although she sinks into a psychotic state at the end, this is hardly an indication that she has never

had the capacity to reason. As for John Givings, the *Atlantic* reviewer seems to be reacting to the rising tide of nonsense in American literary culture about the sanity of the mad. In fact, Yates is not valorizing Givings at all: his demented declaiming rarely sounds more daft than Frank Wheeler's glib living room rhetoric, which is to say that Yates is wise to the hopelessness of mere talk about hopelessness. While it is true that Yates depicts a society that denies the unseemly and the shocking, it is also clear enough that his rebels and protesters are limp and unconvincing as spokesmen for renewal. The beauty of Yates's portraits, like Flaubert's, is to be found in their ironic appropriateness: people's yearnings, Emma Bovary's or the Wheelers's, are achingly real and true to the logic of their lives, but all wrong when measured against the limits of life.

The more incisive responses are unimpeded by pointless questions about Frank and April, their sanity, and their human worth. Several reviewers perceive major inconsistencies in the book's vision of society. The *Saturday Review* critic, after praising Yates for "passion and irony held deftly in balance," brings up a few unanswered questions in the book.[9] How much of the disaster can be accounted for by a bad marriage or bad upbringings? In short, is there any clear causality at work in the narrative? Our answer in this study has been that the dazed Wheelers, immobilized by their own intoxicating and clever rhetoric, have created great expectations over a period of many years that were totally disconsonant with their abilities, their social equipment, and their best interests.

Theodore Solotaroff, a critic who fully understands what's wrong with the Wheelers, takes a similar approach to ours, locating the tragedy in a thinning-out of American class strengths.[10] Frank is the child of a highly competent, hard-working salesman who commanded respect in his world of clients and contacts; his son remembers the masterful way he handled tools when he was pursuing his woodworking on a weekend. Frank has lost touch with that middle-class commitment to a job well done. Scattered and rather ineffectual, he seems to represent the destiny of many children of solid people. According to Solotaroff, April lacks the glitter of her roaring-20s parents: their upper-class style—the clothes, the urbanity, the ease—is just a memory to the girl who yearns for everything that is out of reach. Raised by a punitive aunt, she has never really caught on to the fact that those glamorous people have little to do with her life anymore. With the emphasis on these two losses of class identity, *Revolutionary Road* becomes a document about American letdowns: the strengths and hopes are no longer available.

Yates's epigraph for *Revolutionary Road* is a line from Keats: "Alas! when passion is both meek and wild!" The people in the novel are in the grip of intense desires, yet their passions flag when they are confronted with the arduous task of making them into realities. The self, at once demanding and incapable, is shown in its most diminished forms. Popular culture also knows Keats's truth: just before the 1960s moved into its experiments and protests against human limitation, the musical comedy *Gypsy* gave a line to its protagonist that sums up the frustrations of Yates's people: "Some people sit on their butts/Got the dream, yeah, but not the guts!"[11] Yates's unfashionable interest in the terms of ordinary failure, his ruthless pursuit of the dismal specifications of middle-class catastrophe, makes *Revolutionary Road* a classic of American realism.

Chapter 4

Limitations and Losses:
Eleven Kinds of Loneliness,
Disturbing the Peace, A Good School

At several points in his career, Yates employed the concentrated effect of *Revolutionary Road:* the short stretch of time during which characters lose their emotional bearings and flounder in the American class system. *Eleven Kinds of Loneliness* (1962), all but completed before *Revolutionary Road* appeared in 1961, is a series of classically proportioned stories that deal with people as irreparably damaged as the Wheelers. The book is a map of separations—distances between a coarse husband and his fragile wife, a middle-class teacher and her working-class student, a sophisticated writer and his hopelessly naive collaborator, a chronically ill veteran and his troubled family. In its themes and style, it points the way to the radical separations of *Disturbing the Peace,* a 1975 novel about a pathetically lonely salesman who goes mad in the 1960s. *A Good School,* appearing in 1978, is another pithy treatment of loss, loneliness, and isolation. Its setting, a Connecticut prep school during World War II, creates a circumscribed and intense world like that of the early stories and the novel about madness.

Eleven Kinds of Loneliness has become one of the signature texts of its age. "Mere mention" of its title, a *New York Times* reviewer noted, "is enough to produce quick, affirmative nods from a whole generation of readers." The book is "almost the New York equivalent of *Dubliners.*"[1] Kurt Vonnegut referred to it as "one of the ten best short-story collections ever written by an American."[2] Yates, "the writer's writer," has been showered with such praise for this book, yet he has never secured the general recognition accorded to other realistic writers of his era.[3]

Perhaps this lack of recognition is because the book has moods, landscapes, and characters that dampened the enthusiasm of early 1960s audiences. Yates offers no glamour, no glimmering dreams, no sustained reveries. The interest of the stories does not involve the sex and mayhem and intellectual restlessness of *Revolutionary Road. Eleven Kinds of Loneli-*

ness is about a different 1950s: the flat lives of people who for the most part have never heard of Sartre and don't seem to care that they are mired in routine and conformity.

The book has certain affinities with another classic collection, J. D. Salinger's *Nine Stories*. Yates admired Salinger as a craftsman and seems to have cultivated some of his acreage. Side by side, the volumes constitute two versions of midcentury isolation. Both writers focus on the distances between people: husbands and wives who talk at cross-purposes, children cut off from the adult world, suburbanites and urban misfits trying fitfully to communicate their inner distress, sensitive people dealing with bland philistines. Salinger staked a claim on postwar loneliness some eight years before Yates. His people point the way to Yates's edgy, desperate characters: Seymour Glass in "A Perfect Day for Bananafish" talking on the beach with a small child on the day of his suicide; the narrator of "For Esmé with Love and Squalor" pulling out of a nervous breakdown and thinking of a friendly little English girl; the lachrymose housewife in "Uncle Wiggly in Connecticut" recalling moments from a youthful romance. Yates's characters also are depicted as they sort through the fragments of their lives and try unsuccessfully to leave messages about their own suffering.

Yet the distances between these two writers are considerable. In style Salinger offered Yates little that he chose to develop: the ambiguity of his stories' endings, the looseness of his plots, and the oddball dialogue of his characters are as far as one can get from Yates's plainness. So also is the romantic or spiritual charge in *Nine Stories*. Except for the most obtuse and philistine, Salinger's people tap into a wealth of spiritual sources: Eastern mysticism, nurturing parental love, eccentricity and nonconformity. Yates's *Eleven Kinds of Loneliness* contains no such sustenance. Salinger's characters sometimes reach peaks of insight; Yates's people wander around in a quotidian world.

Anti-Camelot

Appearing at the time of John Kennedy's New Frontier, Yates's stories also read like affronts to vigor. Resignation always outweighs enthusiasm, and youthful ardor is never allowed to run away with the characters' lives. The book is about old frontiers: the individualism, selfishness, complacency, and self-absorption of the Eisenhower years. The misdirected rebelliousness of the Wheelers is even too intense for the characters in this second book: *Revolutionary Road,* after all, explored men and women who were interrogating the terms of their lives; most of the characters in *Eleven Kinds of Loneliness* lack the reflective power to do more than brood and regret.

Yates provides eleven accounts of insufficiency; he studies the effects of habitually failing to know who you are, what it is you can reasonably expect, and why your actions are so awkward and destructive. Loss of identity, futile class assertions, and faulty behavior make the people in the stories into monads that collide and then go off in their lonely directions. The reader is left to calculate the damages. Yates's collection—unlike Joyce's *Dubliners*, Hemingway's *In Our Time*, or Anderson's *Winesburg, Ohio*—has a discursive title, yet it lacks the orderly and explicit working-out of themes of those more famous books. Joyce artfully arranged his stories to survey the varieties of paralysis in modern Ireland; Hemingway wove obvious connecting threads and recounted episodes in the life of Nick Adams; and Anderson hammered home his themes with sententious passages of interior monologue and authorial comment. By contrast, Yates's stories seem like stray bits of reality dropped into book form; they cohere not because of any contrivance but because of Yates's overarching vision.

That vision is one of the bleakest in contemporary American literature. Little guys and women, born, generally, in the 1920s, growing up during the Great Depression, coming of age during the war, are equipped with the feeblest upbeat rhetoric of their time. The hopes and resentments of the little guy, including the sentimental rhetoric of the Popular Front and the anger of World War II infantrymen, are about the most intense emotions in the book. Yates's people find ways of ventilating that express their typical situations as victims of the depression and the war years, small-time partakers in 1950s prosperity.

Diana Trilling has focused on what shaped the sensibility of a typical Popular Front writer of the 1940s who dealt with yearnings and dreams; she chose Stephen Longstreet's *The Land I Live* as an example of "a little man prose, a soft, lilting language of self-effacing decency."[4] Longstreet describes his faith in mankind, especially "the rights of lovers and children and fields" (which of course are being trampled by the fat cats) (D. Trilling, 341). The limp, dispirited quality of this belief is what Yates frequently captures: his America is braced up by nothing stronger than this unconvincing optimism. The Longstreets of the 1940s, with their talk of love and fulfillment in a world made better by ordinary men and women, are often the points of reference in *Eleven Kinds of Loneliness*. Yates shows the irony of such feeble thinking, the desperation of those who have no more to hold on to than vague uplift. When he is not using the hopeful, yearning mode, he often turns to another little-man style, the truculent and resentful tones of the McCarthy era.

His stories are rendered from the points of view of feeble idealists pursuing misconceived plans. The three ideas that emerge are identity loss, class anxiety, and social ineptitude. Yates concentrates his energies on these ideas, with no particular stress on one over the other. Some stories, like the first group considered here, deal with ravages of war and institutional life; but similar raw materials and situations, dealing with army men and schoolchildren in the 1930s, are nevertheless shaped into studies of class anxiety. For his stories about faulty interaction, Yates has concentrated on New York City people who misunderstand their jobs and the demands of their co-workers.

The Diminishment of Identity

"Jody Rolled the Bones" is a highly complex story of discovery and loss. The men in an army platoon learn about the discipline of soldiering from a hard-boiled sergeant; although they are in awe of his talent as a teacher and leader, they never lapse into any sentimental identification with him. But for a time they discover that there is something more worthwhile than a feel-good attitude about your leader; in training they learn that a "thing well-done"—marching, handling a bayoneted rifle— produces intense pleasure and is more satisfying than a fuzzy, warm feeling about the army. Sergeant Reece, a model to his men without being just another pal, offers instruction that is "classically simple": watching him is like watching a heavy hitter select a bat; his precision makes even the officers seem sloppy (11K, 50). On one occasion, when he's pulling himself together after a hangover, he appears late for reveille, yet doesn't receive any reprimand from the lieutenant.

Gruff and something of a martinet, he nevertheless stands forth as a mysterious ideal of excellence: in Yates's world of stumblers, excuse makers, and losers, he is bound to show up those around him. Like the craftsman who ignores the distractions of the world and the opinions of others, he does his job with quiet self-confidence, all the while creating an atmosphere that shames the stupid, the inept, and the sloppy. On one occasion, a cocky private wants to defy Reece by drinking a lot of water on a march. He promptly gets sick. But when the recruits repress their reckless impulses for a time and listen to the hard rules of soldiering, they discover something greater than themselves. And just as they begin to experience the pleasures of exacting work, they also become dimly aware of another of Reece's messages: that what's given can be taken away. Just as they are becoming an efficient platoon, Sergeant Reece is transferred to other duties.

The story's title comes from a marching song about the archetypal civilian, named Jody, who has all the luck in life because of a roll of the dice. Reece has his recruits march to it, and Yates makes them lose all they have to fate and chance and impulse. The men don't quite realize what they have achieved and don't quite realize that a roll of the bones can take it away.

The story's shifts of mood are achieved with remarkable subtlety. Although concerned with a rough group of recruits, the story is actually about their pain and their loss of finer perceptions and sensibilities. In the process of learning from Reece, the men register a variety of responses: rage at his demands, admiration of his talents, disappointment at his aloofness, feelings of entitlement and betrayal, wise-guy denial of his worth. The last response, in which Yates skillfully shows the men holding firmly to their false perceptions and their doubts, constitutes a grim conclusion. Once in pursuit of excellence, the men end up convincing themselves that their new sergeant, an easygoing good Joe named Ruby, is an adequate substitute for a first-rate leader. The platoon, once tense with the excitement of doing its best, becomes "round-shouldered, relieved, and confident" as it accepts mediocrity (*11K*, 58). Mere survival, Ruby's way, is preferable to the rigors of real soldiering. In his characteristic manner, Yates lets false recognitions steal the last scene. Who wants to be professional, anyway? Like the young boy in Joyce's "Araby" who gives up his ardors and dreams—mere vanity, he tells himself—the soldiers have lost their precious sense of achievement. Once a precise and skillful fighting unit, they will be "scattered and absorbed in the vast disorder" of the army (*11K*, 58).

Being swallowed up, losing your distinctive style or skill or sense of yourself, is also the central idea of "No Pain Whatsoever." Here the people have long ago given up on life: Harry Wilson, a depressed and aloof TB patient, keeps all hope at a distance. While making her perfunctory visit to him, his estranged wife, Myra, also gives up trying to believe in their future. Harry, a veteran who has undergone several lung operations, doesn't have anything to say to the new men in the TB ward or to his wife, for that matter. He and the older guys who have undergone a few years of treatment have a tacit understanding, an eerily calm recognition of their fate. New guys, outsiders, wives fail to break through to the core of suffering that unites these men. According to Harry there's actually "no pain whatsoever"—which is to say, nothing to talk about with anyone outside the group. Harry calls Myra "honey," asks her a few formulaic questions about her work, and then proceeds to read a magazine. Myra is also caught up in the allegiances of a group: on the December Sunday of the story's action, she has accepted a ride to the hospital from her friends loudmouthed Marty and giggly Irene. Her crude boyfriend, Jack, is along for the ride. These people are her source of negative reinforcement. They are the equivalent of Harry's old crowd from the ward.

In a cleverly balanced series of scenes—car, hospital, car—Yates dramatizes Harry's and Myra's losses. Harry pretends to be interested in life outside, but submits to his role of invalid. On the drive out, Myra resisted Jack's back seat advances, only to let him have his way after the hospital visit. Impulse overwhelms intention, just as it has in "Jody Rolled the Bones."

The details of the story are arranged for maximum effect: almost everything has to do with shutting out meaning, blocking communication, or covering up. At the hospital, radios blare, making it all but impossible for visitors to hear themselves talk. The men—Harry trying to read *Popular Science,* Red O'Meara blandly saying his wife "comes Saturdays now"—seem not to recognize that it's visiting hours (*11K,* 64). Mrs. Balacheck, the Red Cross volunteer, starts to play "Jingle Bells" on the piano to drown out the sound of departing visitors. The carolers "cough quietly to themselves" until it's time to perform (a gruesomely ironic contrast with the TB patients) (*11K,* 70). Harry, wrapped up in his high-waisted robe, seems totally alien to Myra with her turned-up collar. The only sign of communication is Myra's submission to Jack: she wants to go right home with him after they have a couple of drinks at a roadhouse. Myra's thoughts are also withheld from the reader, making the story starker and more disturbing than a pat narrative about a character who comes-to-realize something.[5]

The other story about hospitalized veterans, "Out with the Old," provides a good example of the way Yates reworks his theme of loss. In fact, this later story is not about defeat at all: instead, it takes people to the brink of destruction and shows the terms of their survival. Its material is dispiriting, but its conclusions are far from grim. A group of TB patients are depicted during the Christmas season, the main action taking place on New Year's Eve. But this time the narrative is laced with humor in the vein of the Three Stooges. Tiny Kovacs, a hulking fellow who fights depression with nonsense and slapstick, has concocted a good midnight skit for the guys on the ward. He will take the part of the newborn baby 1951, if he can get MacIntyre, a skinny bald man with no teeth, to take the part of the old year. MacIntyre is also sunk in depression, brooding on his horrible Christmas at home with his family: his unmarried daughter has become pregnant and is about to collapse with nervous strain; his teenage son is a little wise guy with a greasy pompadour and no respect for anyone. In short, he is in no mood for Tiny's nonsense.

Tiny himself is recovering from an encounter with the outside world: at his home in Queens he is a respected and loved figure, but he cannot help feeling the distance that separates him from ordinary healthy people. All the men brood about their divided lives and seem to know quite well that they no longer have a place on the outside. When they get dressed to go home for Christmas, they don't quite recognize each other. Each becomes a curious version of himself, a Yale man, a prosperous Queens restaurant owner's son. Yet each knows he will come back, like a Cinderella of the postwar era, and be transformed into a pathetic figure in pajamas.

MacIntyre breaks the pattern of misery by abandoning a futile scheme to take his daughter away to the country; instead he decides to tear up a letter to the girl and, for a night at least, accept one of Tiny's schemes. He chooses life, renewal, and camaraderie, rather than the problems of the old year. The lonely men will enjoy their smuggled whiskey and their prank; they will forget about the insoluble conflicts outside the hospital and the deadening waiting game within. Tiny—to the outside world Harold, a man at once dignified in his Christmas bathrobe and infantile as he clowns among his fellow patients with a quacking rubber duck—is Yates's survivor and delight maker. His characterization is perilously close to sentimentality, especially when he breaks down at Christmas with his little niece in his arms. But Yates's sense of the ironic and the off-key makes the scene a fine evocation of middle-class life. The little girl tells God to make Uncle Harold well: "You shunt *tell* him. You should *ask* him," Harold says (*11K,* 176). Altogether, Tiny and MacIntyre and the others claim moments of escape and pleasure in two settings of loss and loneliness—home and hospital. But the hospital seems to be the privileged place, and it seems much more sensible to be Tiny and avoid the strain of being Uncle Harold. One can only bear to live among momentary pleasures and adopted roles.

But even the attempt to make the best of an inhospitable world fails in "Fun with a Stranger." The setting is a classroom and the victims are children constrained and unsettled by a sour, punishing teacher with the unfortunate name Miss Snell.[6] Both the children and their teacher are portrayed with great subtlety: instead of creating bored kids and a monstrously authoritarian teacher, Yates gives the reader a perceptive group of boys and girls who are looking for redeeming qualities in an unpromising person. All along they have been told that Miss Snell is no Miss Cleary, the latter a cheerful, attractive young woman. Nevertheless, the children are sensitive to the complexities and ambiguities of the adult world. After all, Miss Snell does demonstrate a certain goodwill; she has a curious way of suggesting that the class is destined to blossom into something exciting. She wants to "make the effort" to know her students because "you can't very well have fun with a stranger" (*11K*, 117). Her faint, homely smile and her vague promises of a Christmas party make the students defensive about her. Yates cleverly makes their allegiance into something vaguely embarrassing: you can't condemn her, but you can't feel comfortable about praising her either. Like others in Yates's fiction, the pupils are caught between conflicting responses (recall April Wheeler's feelings about Frank or the recruits' reactions to Sergeant Reece) and are at the mercy of a mysterious force, in this case a neurotic loser who wants to survive in a job.

The story, in all its dispiriting brilliance, is dependent on two special occasions, a class trip and the Christmas party that it seems to foreshadow. Both are misfires for Miss Snell. The trip is a dismal, although quite comically rendered excursion to the town where steam locomotives are changed to electric; it highlights the teacher's inability to hold the students' interest. While Miss Cleary can transform the boring facts about locomotives into exciting lessons, Miss Snell can only insist that the students stay together in a group. In her old black coat and hat, poor Miss Snell, like the shapeless eraser that she prides herself on always having at hand, looks lumpy; Miss Cleary is a vibrant presence with long hair and a polo coat. On the day before the Christmas recess, Miss Snell delivers her final devastating blow to the students: the only sign of the holidays is a miserable gift for each child—an eraser. The loss is total: the children can no longer maintain their tolerant illusions. The dynamics of Yates's world, corresponding to Erving Goffman's account of sustained and ruined dramatic scenes, are clear enough: there is nothing for the children to do but run off, without any discussion, when school is dismissed.

Stories of Class Conflict

A second type of story in the volume—exemplified by "Doctor Jack-o'-Lantern," "The Best of Everything," "The B.A.R. Man," and "A Really Good Jazz Piano"—is pervaded by ideas of social class. Yates covers the terrain of American class, ranging from the bafflement of a slum kid, to the frustrations of the lower-middle-class office worker, to the complacencies of middle-class teachers and children, to the snobberies of Yalies at play in the south of France. Each story has its conflict involving social position, esteem, and claims to respect and happiness. And each is about people who panic when they are confronted with the realities of class. When the characters are challenged by people outside their class or brought face to face with the limits of their position, they fail to maintain their dignity or win themselves any credit. In Erving Goffman's terms, their "virtual reality"—what they want to project—is overwhelmed by their "actual reality": deficiencies of manner and behavior that stigmatize them.[7]

Vincent Sabella, the protagonist of "Doctor Jack-o'-Lantern," is a working-class character who is immersed in such problems. Generally Yates deals with lower-middle-class people and fumbles a bit when confronted with the world of the very poor, the struggling mass of survivors who have no access to middle class values and illusions. Usually, he can only sketch the lives of the deprived. But Vincent is the exception. A castoff of the New York City welfare system, the boy finds himself in a suburban public school in 1941, a foster child thrown in with children who seem untouched by the misery of the depression. The story deals with the yawning gap that separates the socially secure from the mysterious members of the underclass. Yates's situations are starkly contrasted and rather raw: the ragged, resentful child of poverty collides with smug children and a do-gooder teacher. At first one is tempted to imagine that Yates is recycling aspects of the 1937 movie *Dead End,* based on the Sidney Kingsley play about slum kids encountering an East Side Manhattan rich boy. But the rather crude vision of the movie is nothing like Yates's handling of American class conflict: unlike the stereotypical street kid, Vincent exhibits a range of emotions that reflect the larger problem of class in America.

When he enters the classroom as the new boy, the scene echoes Charles Bovary's first day at school in *Madame Bovary.* The kids stare at this lower-class phenomenon, and Yates uses the omniscient "you" to read the middle-class mind; this "you" includes the kids, their teacher, and the reader. (And by the end of the story "you," the reader, will be made quite uncomfortable, as a queasy sense of guilt and a recognition of complacency set in.) But meanwhile, Vincent was not from the part of New York that "swallowed up fathers every day" and that you visited occasionally in your best clothes. "You had to pass through his New York" on the train—"the part where people hung bedding over their windowsills and leaned out on it all day in a trance of boredom." His dress and voice ("hoarse" from yelling down "ugly streets") and the name Vinny are marks of woe that elicit faint smiles from the boys and giggles from the girls (*11K,* 4). And the teacher, Miss Price, is hardly more sensitive or aware of Vinny's perspective. She tries to praise his artwork, "be friends" (recall Miss Snell), and talk with him. But like many a Yates character, she stumbles over her words ("what I mean is") and conveys the wrong impression. Poor Vinny is very aware of her "slim stockinged foot" and "her long thighs" (*11K,* 10–11). In a sense she is Miss Cleary transplanted into another story: a well-meaning pretty woman who helps others to build up the wrong set of expectations.

The story is about basic misunderstandings and denials on both sides of the class divide. Vinny is never going to understand middle-class kids' or teachers' references, signals, and values. Take, for example, the hit movie *Dr. Jekyll and Mr. Hyde,* a pop culture touchstone for kids in the early 1940s. The picture is the subject of discussion in Miss Price's class. One twit named Nancy wasn't allowed to see it, but nevertheless uses it as an excuse to go on about her brother, his college roommate, and her sister's wedding; two boys have seen it and would like to discuss the sensational stuff, but here again the subject is cut short, this time by Miss Price. Vinny has obviously learned what should be on his mind: on the next Monday he comes in with a report on "Doctor Jack-o'-Lantern," complete with preposterous details and his own equivalent of Nancy's what-I-did-on-the-weekend. He tells a whopper about his mudda and fodda and a cop who chased their car and exchanged gunfire. The kids view this with scorn and regard him as a circus freak. At lunchtime Miss Price tells him he would have done better to tell about the purchase of his new windbreaker.

Just as she understands nothing of his world, he cannot swallow her nauseating niceties. In a symbolic scene after the talk, Vinny vomits and thereafter lets his lust and frustration take over as he chalks up dirty words on a school wall. The irony is compounded when the kids discover the transgression. They think he will get hell, but actually he gets more bland advice from Miss Price; they think he will back off and be contrite, but he starts acting like Edward G. Robinson in *Little Caesar*. Miss Price keeps telling herself that "Vincent" will soon adjust to the class. True to the pattern that Yates often uses, the story shows her walking off in a smug middle-class daze. She takes pleasure in greeting Vincent, complimenting his warm windbreaker, and telling herself that everything is going to be all right. The latter phrase always signals catastrophe in Yates. In this case it foreshadows Vinny's final devastating rejection of suburban niceness. Yates's pattern, whether the story is about loss, class, or clumsiness, almost always involves a blow to people's ideas of dignity and order. In this story, the shock comes as the humiliated and enraged boy, trying "in vain to retain his dignity," further abases himself (*11K*, 19). He draws an obscene picture of Miss Price, an expression of his thwarted sexual feelings and impotent toughness.

Throughout the story Yates has probed the mind of the boy without quite entering it. Unlike Miss Price, the narrator does not try to be understanding in the way of the child psychologist. He emphasizes signals rather than trying to explain motivations. Vinny comes across in his body language, his furtive glances, his immediate reactions to the kids and the teacher. Yates sets up conflicting bourgeois and proletarian systems, and lets the reader sort out the meagerness of each. Danger to Warren Berg and Bill Stringer is using a backyard swing made of a rubber tire; to Vinny it's a shoot-out with the cops. Status for the kids involves being cool and judgmental and often silent; to Vinny it's the swagger of a gangster. The defining experience for a middle-class child is socializing in somebody else's house; for Vinny it's being alone in the alley or on his imaginary highway. Among the types in Yates's volume, Vinny seems isolated by his faulty (and at times comical) array of status indicators. Only his windbreaker keeps him warm in suburbia. As readers we are left, necessarily, outside Vinny's world, able to see Miss Price for what she is, but forced to see some of ourselves in her. Yates has trapped us in the quagmire of class.

"The Best of Everything" and "The B.A.R. Man" are about lower-middle-class people whose miseries are less extreme than Vinny's. In the former story Grace and Ralph, two office workers, are captured on the eve of their wedding. Yates makes them victims of their environment: Ralph, the guy from Sunnyside, Queens, who has never moved beyond the aspirations of the crowd at the local bar; Grace, the Pennsylvania mill town girl who is essentially bewildered by her new life in Manhattan and the attitudes of her college-educated roommate.

The defeat depicted here is quiet but devastating. Two people learn that they have little to offer each other, and that there is no way to compensate for their inadequacies. Grace, who has never been quite sure whether she knew Ralph well enough or too well, has decided that this is the night to put on a nylon negligee and make love to him. But no sooner has she fortified herself with dry sherry, the upper-middle-class roommate's drink, than Ralph arrives full of beer and in a state of non-romantic excitement. His buddies have given him a bachelor party, and he can stay with Grace only a few minutes. He snaps at her when she tries to detain him; she smiles tiredly as she sees him off. The counter-pointing here is Yates at his most precise, and the effect makes the reader recall crucial details. It turns out that Ralph is exactly what the snobbish roommate dismissed him as: a little white worm, incapable of anything more substantial than barroom banter ("Hey, wha' happen t'ya Giants?") and sentimentality (*11K*, 26).

Yates has designed a hard fate for Ralph: every aspect of his character is at once self-protective and pathetic. Ostensibly his big moment with Grace was the time they danced and he sang "Easter Parade" softly to her. But actually we know that the high point of their relationship is his nights out with his friend Eddie: talking about his dates is more fun than the complications of a relationship. Better than Grace's nylon negligee is the leather overnight bag that the guys give him as a going-away present: at one time he seemed to be interested in sex, but by the eve of the wedding he much prefers a gift that reminds him of his simple past. Grace, certainly the more mature and reflective of the two, smiles and spends time wondering about him. Ralph isn't thinking much about her at all. Grace's smile, the gestural equivalent of "everything will be all right," is of course a dismal smile of resignation. The next day they are going off to be married, not to each other as much as to their old habits and class identities.

"The B.A.R. Man" uses the same class notation, this time to describe the fate of a married couple. John Fallon and his wife, Rose, are what Ralph and Grace are sure to become. They seem to be everything that the educated middle class fears most: when not trapped in their unfulfilling jobs, they argue in a domestic setting of china figurines. Like Ralph, Fallon would really prefer to be out with his buddies rather than with his wife; Rose, skinny and childless because of a tipped uterus, would like to break Ralph's Friday night routine with the crowd at a bar and get him to accompany her to a movie.

Each partner has a short fuse, and each has outbursts of temper that give the story its shape. No one at work understands Fallon's boastful, truculent talk about his army days and the beauty of the Browning Automatic Rifle (the B.A.R. of the title). He snaps at his co-workers' ignorant questions and gives them a condescending lecture about the weapon (which he in fact fired only twice). At home that night his temper flares again: he spars with Rose, making nasty fun of her padded bra and dredging up the question of children. She has given up the prescribed exercises for her condition, obviously because Fallon isn't much of an earner. They slash at each other's ego for a while, and Fallon soon slams the door and leaves her flat on Gregory Peck night at the local movie house.

After he hits a few Manhattan bars and tries to get a respectful hearing from strangers, Fallon discovers that he can't lose his rage and frustration, even when out in a crowd. His B.A.R. line helps him to tag along for the evening with two soldiers and pick up some women; but when he tries to impress a sexy Italian girl from the Bronx (who is as bored and unresponsive as Rose), he winds up being ditched by the group. Alone and fuming, like a not-so-adult version of Vincent Sabella, he needs to assert his power. Since two women and several men have rejected him in one day, he looks for someone to humiliate. Down in the Village he happens on just the right person: a communist lawyer named Mitchell, a victim of the McCarthy hearings, is at the center of a noisy demonstration and seems like the perfect punching bag.

If it weren't for Fallon's carefully built-up resentment, the scene that follows would be overblown: but Yates is able to pull off a conclusion in which Fallon viciously attacks this class enemy of the average guy. Earlier on Fallon heard a man on the street saying, "Maybe you can argue with McCarthy's methods, but son of a bitch, you can't argue with him on principle" (*11K, 136*). The irony of the remark hits the reader with full force: Fallon's methods for working off his grudge are revolting and his "principle"—a macho love of domination—is equally unattractive. Fallon's snarling and bullying is also a small-time version of McCarthy's swaggering. Like the senator, Fallon is proud of being a plain guy, is fed up with people who don't see his truths, and is ready to brand them as weaklings or snobs.

Yates's descriptions of the communist intellectuals who accompany Mitchell—snobbish men, "petulant" girls in black slacks—keeps the story from being a wholesale attack on the ill-favored Fallon. The class markers that make him look like a typical tough (the "gas blue" shiny suit, the shoes with steel-capped heels) are balanced off by the indicators that make Mitchell look like a typical Village radical (the cheap tweed suit). Yates has mercy for no one here or elsewhere in the story. Rose Fallon appears in a hideous wrapper and ludicrous high heels; the guys from the office are as ignorant as Fallon says they are. Everyone makes the kind of bad appearance that constitutes the outward sign of inward gracelessness. The only grace and dignity available is to be found in the memory of the Browning Automatic itself. Like the men in "Jody Rolled the Bones," Fallon once knew something of the fine discipline of handling a weapon well. But in trying to rekindle the excitement of the previous decade, Fallon entangles himself in his worst impulses: a blustering tough rather than a tough warrior, he is a ridiculous victim of the class war.

Yates follows that war into the regions of the American upper class in "A Really Good Jazz Piano." The story is his only early exploration of money and leisure; but in its mordant portrayal of two Yale graduates, it points the way to the false and incoherent world of inherited wealth in *A Special Providence, A Good School,* and *Young Hearts Crying.* The two pals in the story seem to emerge from F. Scott Fitzgerald's "The Rich Boy." They partake of Anson Hunter's massive confusion: as they take stock of their place in the modern world, they find themselves bewildered, humiliated, and alone.

Cannes, the only glamorous place in *Eleven Kinds of Loneliness,* is the setting for one of the most skillfully rendered social catastrophes in the Yates's oeuvre. Carson Wyler and Ken Platt—the first a sophisticate, the second his insecure sidekick—are reunited when Ken phones his friend in Paris and cajoles him into coming south on the pretext that he must hear a great pianist named Sid. Seemingly a bit annoyed by the sidekick's interference in his life, Carson nevertheless says hello to Sid and invites him to join the IBF, The International Bar Flies Club. The rest of the story is about the uneasy relations between leisured people and the hard-working black man.[8] Almost Jamesian in the way it studies the ironies of character, the story focuses on Ken and Carson's evaluations of Sid's limitations; such concentration in turn brings their own faults into high relief.

Ken begins by claiming that the crucial thing about Sid is his authenticity; he has built a life for himself in a country that does not condescend to people of color. But these rich-boy pronouncements are part of a chain of deception in the story, and indeed in *Eleven Kinds of Loneliness* as a whole. As Yates scrutinizes the collision of class and race, everyone comes off badly: the characters try to dignify themselves but wind up embarrassed. Ken and Carson reevaluate Sid and conclude that, after all, he is not so great: he's trying to make a living and has been playing up to Murray Diamond, a Las Vegas promoter who comes to the little club where Sid works. He also seems to be performing like some stereotypical black. As Sid adapts his playing and singing for Vegas taste, Ken and Carson become censorious. Forgetting their own privilege and judging Sid by some Olympian standard, they make themselves petty. At one point Sid wants to demonstrate his chumminess with Carson (perhaps in a phony way because Diamond is looking on); he gives the Yalie the barfly signal—"bzz-z-z bzz-z-z" and a tap on the lapel. But Carson snubs him: barflies, apparently, must be free of any social stains, must be gentlemen who don't make up to Vegas hustlers. It's creditable, evidently, to waste time, drink, and comment on other people's quality; it's discreditable to soil oneself in the marketplace. According to such reasoning, blacks also do well when they conform to the snobbish pattern of expatriate artists; they degrade themselves when they try to make a better living.

Yates uses Sid's story to explore one of his favorite themes: the phoniness and exclusivism that often surrounds the figure of the artist. Actually, Carson and Ken know nothing about music; their judgments are the kinds of vague generalities and clichés that Yates is always highlighting. As for Sid, he too is implicated in their world of pretense: why, we might ask, isn't he wise to these losers? Or if he is wise, why does he want to profit from being associated with them? In Yates's social imbroglios, the reader can never quite separate integrity from duplicity, sincerity from playacting. We get the sense that the luckless Ken has overdramatized Sid's qualities to improve his status with his friend; in a very real sense, this surely takes us back to Frank Wheeler and the stagy scenes devised to impress April.

Altogether the story is a classic exploration of the terms of self-assertion and class pride. In its picture of warped whites with money setting up standards for blacks and being shocked when they are confronted with the realities of black existence, the story reminds the reader of the main theme of Ellison's *Invisible Man:* beware of people's social interpretations of you.

As the two snobs exit from the club after the "barfly" rebuff, Carson maintains a studied dignity while Ken displays a "flabby," quavering smile. With stunning virtuosity and economy Yates reverses their roles in the final scene. Proud Carson is quite diminished; sidekick Ken realizes the horrible thing that they have done. They have discredited themselves as gentlemen and men of the world and descended to the level of bigots. The dynamics of the failure are similar to those in Goffman's *Pre-*

sentation of Self in Everyday Life: the refusal to give the barfly signal is a careless lapse, what Goffman calls an "unmeant gesture" that is intended to assert classiness, but that actually reveals the pique and jealousy of the petty snob; cutting Sid spoils Carson's performance (Goffman 1959, 51). It's too late, however, for anything but denial and escape. As the two have to pass the entrance to the bar a second time, we are made to feel all their shame; Sid's music "comes up loud" to mock them.

Faulty Behavior

Another group of stories concentrates on people who are chronically inept. The quality of these pieces is uneven, ranging from the one-joke story "A Glutton for Punishment" to the clever schtick of "A Wrestler with Sharks" to the searching character study of "Builders." These New York tales of schemers and losers have more humor than Yates usually exhibits, but the first two are also a bit predictable. "A Glutton for Punishment," the weakest piece in the volume, gives some weight to the critic Peter Buitenhuis's dismissive comments about Yates's formulas: in the story of a businessman's collapse, Yates seems to give away the weakness too soon. Walter Henderson, a genteel failure who has just lost his latest job, is always described in terms of falls.[9] The only time he has ever ascended was on the day that he climbed up the New York Public Library steps on Fifth Avenue to meet his future wife. His interest as a character comes from his mysterious desire, reminiscent of April Wheeler's, to assume roles and play them badly. On the day that Walter gets the sack, he goes through a host of gestural gymnastics meant to maintain his dignity; he offsets his real life by busying himself with such details as getting to the elevator in his office building without belying his new condition of joblessness, taking the long route home in order not to arrive too early.

Again Erving Goffman's ideas of protecting one's image are crucial here: in *Stigma* Goffman deals with Henderson's kind of problem (Goffman 1963, 17). The hidden wound—chronic failure that has now taken the form of joblessness—is something that Henderson wants to keep "backstage" in his life; in Yates's story we are mostly in Goffman's "backstage" watching Henderson shape his image and find attractive and socially acceptable ways to screw up (Goffman 1959, 112). At the end of the story Yates has Henderson collapse in front of his wife like a performing little boy; this, we are to believe, was the most "graceful" (which is to say successfully orchestrated) thing he had done all day. His posture at the end is so self-conscious that Yates calls it "eloquent" (*11K, 92*).

Yates is funnier and more penetrating on the subject of performers when he depicts Leon Sobel in "A Wrestler with Sharks." Here a little guy with literary and intellectual pretensions gets a job on a labor newspaper after spending years as a sheet metal worker. He is the perfect mouthpiece for Popular Front ideas about how-it-all-looks-from-down-here. Sobel's clumsy forays into writing are related by a younger, well-educated man, someone quite above the level of the rough customers who write plain accounts of labor issues for the paper. Such a narrator has the genial contempt for dreary writing and awful surroundings that Yates must have had for the offices of his early days. He portrays the paper's owners as grudging in their attitude toward the staff, and the staff as most often worthy of the bad treatment that they get.

But Leon Sobel is a breath of absurdity in this tedious setting. While the owners and staff are literal minded, Sobel is an egoist and nudnik, the author of nine unpublished books. Standing between the pedestrian and the absurd is the narrator, the genuine literary man. His eye ranges over the two mentalities and evaluates each with wit. A typical *Labor Leader* writer such as Finney is flat and predictable: his pathetic Broadway column (complete with comments about the class of the new "thrush" at the Copa) is within the bounds of everyday mediocrity; but when Sobel gets a chance to write a gossip column, he produces an unintentionally hilarious personal essay. His flippancy, factitious informality, and uncalled-for candor make him like other clumsy artist figures in Yates, especially the mother in *A Special Providence* and in "Oh, Joseph, I'm So Tired" in *Liars in Love*. He is also touchy and temperamental about his work; his downfall—staged by himself and including a dramatic exit—is a comic complement to Walter Henderson's last day at work. Sobel and Henderson relish their fates.

Yates's best story of bungling has the ironic title "Builders." Yates once again describes a real writer confronting the problem of working with a ludicrous amateur. The first-person narrator is a literary novice (like Yates himself in the late 1940s) who has worked as a rewrite man for the United Press, dreamed of Hemingway's career, and actually groomed an emerging talent. He answers a newspaper ad for a talented writer and thereafter gets involved with a taxi driver who wants to tell his life story. Bernie Silver, a cabby who is a notch or two above Leon Sobel in intelligence, is another fantasizer who dreams of literary glory. Unlike Sobel he's practical and crafty in the way he handles people: he wants to give Bob Prentice weekly writing assignments, basic plot situations to be developed. But when it comes to paying, he stiffs Bob and tries to impress him with talk of his big movie and literary connections. Instead of bragging about nine unpublished books, he tells stories about a school pal, Wade Manley (modeled on the film actor John Garfield), and a former teacher, D. Alexander Corvo, a popular psychologist. He also claims to be connected with "those *New York Times* names, the kinds of which tens of thousands of people are dimly aware" (*11K*, 196–67). He tells Bob that together they can build a best-selling icon from the life of plain Bernie Silver. Flaunting his regular-working-stiff credentials, Bernie uses his charms and pushes Bob further and further into lying and exaggerating.

At first Bob can't bear to assume the little-guy persona; but after a while he learns how to build, which is to say that he writes stories about basic decency and racial tolerance (when in fact Bernie and his wife make snide remarks about "the brown hordes" in the Bronx; *11K*, 214). Bob is in the awkward position of building illusions rather than discovering truths; at crucial points he breaks down. In one loopy scene he gets drunk and sick and tired of being the little guy; he starts to talk of all the money he and Bernie will make and how they will stand up to those *Times* names and slap Lionel Trilling around and demand that Reinhold Niebuhr put up or shut up. This manic episode perfectly captures the idiocy of two deluded men trying to build a house (the story's central metaphor) out of clichés. Bob, who yearned for the dignity of the early Hemingway, has been caught in a world of sloppy sentimentality. He wants to live up to the demands of his craft, but, as his wife reminds him, he should be trying to meet Bernie's demands for Irving Berlin–like schmaltz.

Bob is one of a number of Yates characters who are impaled on Berlin's lyrics. "Easter Parade," for example, is the song that Ralph sings to Grace when they are about to experience "the best of everything" (once intended to be titled "I'll Be All in Clover," a notable lyric from the song); later the Berlin tune highlights the misery of the Grimes sisters in *The Easter Parade*. Bob's entrapment lasts until he has his second manic episode: completely disgusted by the childishness and philistinism of Bernie's plans, he writes a story that travesties Bernie's little-guy-triumphant vision. Here a benign politician gives enormous handouts to the little guys of this world. The story is a dig at Bernie for not paying Bob's fees and a sarcastic reworking of movie material, perhaps Frank Capra's wonderful life of generosity and basic decency. In any case, the bad story signals the end of the collaboration because Bernie takes offense at the lampooning of his sentiments. But there is still building to do. Bob's story, rather than Bernie's, needs development. After lying for so long, he faces the truth: that he has failed to build two of his own novels well, that his marriage has collapsed, and that his fantasies about Hemingway contain as little value as Bernie's nonsense. And the greatest truth is that Bernie's metaphor is the thing that Bob most needs, a way of viewing his own limitations: "I'm not even sure if there are any windows in this particular house" (*11K,* 230). The writer is caught in the unavoidable confusions of life, including his ambivalent feelings about strugglers like Bernie. He says that his truth is "going to have to come in as best it can, through whatever chinks and cracks have been left in the builder's faulty craftsmanship" (*11K,* 230).

From Bernie's schemes to Bob's higher aspirations, all the talk about craftsmanship makes the story into a daft, offbeat meditation on the artist's fate. Disdainful of highfalutin aesthetic discussions, Yates has again brought the topic of art into the poignant realm of human failure. Bernie's strivings contain the seeds of creativity: "Sillier things than that have built empires in America" (*11K,* 229). The awkwardness of both Bernie and Bob, schemer and writer, contains an essential Yates message: whenever life seems merely ludicrous, it starts to turn sad.

Yates's Underground Man

Yates waited years before using the concentrated techniques of *Eleven Kinds of Loneliness* again. During the 1960s he published *A Special Providence,* a ramshackle account of his childhood with his mother and his experiences as an army man in World War II. But with *Disturbing the Peace* he returned to a compact form and a precise problem. The book concerns the tragic social ineptitude of advertising man John Wilder, his road to the madhouse, and the phony people who speed his way there.

Books about madness constituted a veritable industry in the 1960s. Many of them had the same focus as Yates's social study of insanity. From Foucault's *Madness and Civilization,* a classic historical analysis of systems that define madness, to tracts by Thomas Szasz and R. D. Laing on modern society's "manufacture" of madness, 1960s writers and theoreticians turned from depth psychology to the politics and social issues that surround our ideas of mental illness. Kesey's *One Flew Over the Cuckoo's Nest* is of course the signature work of "madness" fiction of the period. Yates was in tune with some of the major currents of thought, but his attitude toward his subject matter was quite different from that of his contemporaries. Cool and analytic, never preachy or polemical, he studied the specifications of his character's downfall without thundering at the sane society. He looked at the mad and the normal and showed how they made up one world of clumsiness, compromise, and hypocrisy.

John Wilder is taken apart piece by piece: we come to see him as the product of faulty social conditioning, bad timing, and physiological destiny. As a child he was a poor reader who never received help and therefore drifted into his own nowhere world of pop culture and media. His snobbish parents never got over his flunking out of Yale. They never got him to appreciate or profit from the family business and its hoity-toity product, Marjorie Wilder's Chocolates. His wife never quite understood that he couldn't read the books she enjoyed. He also was of Mickey Rooney stature in the era of the tall Kennedys, a fact that bedevils him every time he enters an Irish bar and sees the President's image. His abilities as a salesman are often sustained by charm, liquor, and spontaneity rather than any definable skill. Altogether, he's a man with stigmata, visible and hidden, and small talents. His struggles are like those described by Goffman in *Stigma,* his classic study of branded people: trying to "pass" among the better endowed, trying to hide the actual reality of his life behind the virtual reality of his salesman's bonhomie (Goffman 1959, 73–91).

Strangely enough, this tormented man—jealous of the Kennedys' Camelot and the swingers of the 1960s, stuck in the 1950s gray-flannel-suit world while others are following gurus and enjoying Ingmar Bergman—is not rendered in psychological terms. With the spite, pettiness, and envy of Dostoyevsky's *Notes from the Underground* at hand, Yates instead turns outward and scrutinizes the dynamics of poor social performance. The chapters are episodes from the life of a man who loses his dignity when he should be baring his soul. Yates stages catastrophes for Wilder, but gives hardly any interior monologue to express the anguish: the cause of his breakdowns seems to be that his stock of illusions and routines is very poor and his audiences of "normal" friends are always slightly ahead of him; unlike Frank and April Wheeler or the other big-time dreamers, he has a limited repertoire and an unlimited thirst for alcohol. But like Walter Henderson in "A Glutton for Punishment," he seems always to have been falling down.

The book's relationship to Yates's life is telling. Richard Yates and John Wilder both battled alcoholism and family pretensions. But *Dis-*

turbing the Peace introduces another unhappy drinker in the character of Chester Pratt, the author of a daring 1960s novel called *Burn All Your Cities*. Wilder and Pratt, the noncreative and creative drunks, are played against each other in the course of the narrative. DeWitt Henry has remarked that Yates, who spent his own Labor Day in Bellevue, was nevertheless stone cold sober there and capable of looking at both sides of himself: Wilder and Pratt were what he observed (DH interview).

An Anatomy of Madness

The first sections of *Disturbing the Peace* prepare the way for the confrontation between these two versions of the drinker. Wilder has gone through hell during a Labor Day weekend in 1961: committed to Bellevue after a psychotic episode, he has faced the raw facts of his own craziness; yet like an inmate in any asylum, he denies his self-destructive behavior. As the plot unfolds, he uses his charm and his gruesome story to impress a rich and glamorous young woman named Pamela Hendricks (has Yates recalled Walter Henderson in this new tale of total collapse?); together they conceive a plan for making Wilder's weekend of horror into a screenplay. Wilder's final downfall comes when he and Pamela go to Hollywood with their script, an arty version of Wilder's story that was concocted by a group of young people in Vermont. A big producer says the script needs complete overhauling by a fine writer; he recommends Chester Pratt, as it happens, a onetime speech writer for RFK with whom Pamela has had an affair.

The dynamics of humiliation tell a great deal about Yates's life and art. Wilder/Yates is degraded by Pratt/Yates; the Mickey Rooney with no education and no real skill is conquered by the highbrow artist who has written a controversial novel. Wilder drinks and careens; Pratt switches to lemon Coke and makes great money writing Wilder's story for the movies. The book becomes, among other things, a series of messages that Yates is sending to himself. He braces himself up with the idea that a touch of Kennedy glamour, a great first novel, and a prepossessing appearance can beat down the ordinariness of his early life and the anguish of his drinking days. Letting John Wilder perish is like expunging the vulnerabilities of his own nature. As a novel *Disturbing the Peace* also carries a protest against the dreary lives of *Eleven Kinds of Loneliness:* Chester Pratt, who is as much of a wreck as anyone in the Yates canon, can prevail. All he needs to do is write, stay away from drink, and go off with the girl.

Now, the aesthetic problems of this cautionary drama are considerable. The conflict between the two sides of Yates is cleverly worked through, but it is rather predictable and even circular. Craftsmen are destined to end up well; drunken hucksters will hit bottom and stay there. The book has the I-told-you-so quality characteristic of Yates's weaker stories. It all but invites the comment that the born loser is a bad protagonist. And its strongest element, the self-hater's agony and self-consciousness, is damaged by a certain smugness in tone.

The Feigning Game

Nevertheless, Yates is able to do a great deal with Wilder's painful downfall. The book is structured into a chain of falsehoods, phony performances, and sustained pretenses. Even though John seems clownish, the normal people are distinguishable from him only because of their bland conventionality. They are as neurotic, weak, and deficient in insight as the madman, yet they survive because they are better actors and have adjusted well to the malformed script of their jobs and social lives. As he writes about the 1960s, Yates adopts the counterculture's view of normals. Simplistic spouses, do-nothing psychoanalysts, smarmy AA members, kindly (and lecherous) old professors, rationalizing lawyers: a complete list of phonies in the book would include just about every supporting character. And when there is an exception, as in the case of the loudmouthed Doctor Spiegel, who is the star patient in Bellevue, that character seems doomed: despite his truth-telling and wise-guy criticisms of the mental health system, Spiegel has done no more than get himself incarcerated for Labor Day.

But once you learn the game of feigning, you're bound to spend your days in agreeable, mindless cooperation with your fellow pretenders. At Bellevue the head nurse, Charlie, burlesques this bland niceness and adds his own curious mock gentility to the act: in dealing with the insane, he assumes the role of a gentleman among gentlemen, even when his charges are using vile language and otherwise disturbing the peace. John Wilder's wife uses her simpler form of denial; her strained phrases about John's recovery, particularly her "Enormous Pride," are a part of an act that helps to drive John crazier (*DTP,* 93). And John's lawyer and friend Paul Borg also helps to grease the mechanism of hypocrisy; always the solid family man, he nevertheless enjoys a hide-away on Varick Street where he and John have brought girls.

After the Bellevue episode, the book becomes a series of false scenes, episodes that exacerbate John's condition by attempting to cover it up.

The psychoanalytic community is portrayed in all its obtuseness and callousness. Sessions with Dr. Jules Blomberg, "an inattentive pink-eyed audience of one," are exercises in futility for Wilder: his time is up and his curiosity about his psyche is unsatisfied (*DTP,* 105). Indifferent Blomberg foreshadows another distracted practitioner, Dr. Chadwick. Like John Givings's doctor in *Revolutionary Road,* he is portrayed in terms of his tacky habits (eating little candies while consulting) and uncaring attitude. The one doctor who seems capable of real thinking puts John on antidepressants and cuts the talk altogether: it hardly needs to be said that Yates has abruptly closed the discussion of healing with words.

Words, in fact, are almost always ludicrous or disgusting travesties of human truths. Yates includes the uplift of Alcoholics Anonymous in his scathing exploration of clichés in America. His usual strategy is to sour the trite expression or otherwise poison the reader's mind. At one AA meeting that John Wilder attends we hear about lighting one candle rather than cursing the darkness; but for poor John the application means only that Paul Borg is burning a light down on Varick with his latest conquest. AA members are depicted as ham actors and exhibitionists who trip themselves up with their own ridiculous rhetoric. They also love talk for its own sake and so earn a place of scorn in the novel: they should be seen alongside the loquacious fools and self-deluders in all of Yates's books.

The windy wisdom and high-flown rhetoric can also be found at Marlowe College in Vermont, Pamela's alma mater. Here we get clichés about human relationships from the 1960s students and guru pronouncements from old Professor Epstein. This stretch of the novel defines Yates's attitude toward 1960s counterculture. As we have seen, he endorses the radical idea that the mental health system is fraudulent; but he has little taste for the social arrangements and values of the dissident young. The figure of Chester Pratt, the wreck as conqueror rather than the dissident as savior, seems to say it all: old-fashioned 1950s disaffection is better than anything countercultural. Cool detachment is better than rage, and silence is better than explanations.

Yates's anger takes the form of several set pieces that present the cruelty and indifference of institutions and individuals. At the beginning there is Bellevue, a grotesque place where Wilder and his like are tormented by sadistic nurses who enjoy exerting power over their victim-charges. Later on, Hollywood provides the sadism: a smug producer named Munchen actually helps to create a hell on earth for Wilder by having his romantic rival Pratt write a script about the total annihilation of one man's identity. Hollywood, once a place of escape and entertainment, becomes a locale for savage exposure. And like the treatment in Bellevue or a session with an analyst, the movie business pursues its inhumane enterprise with phony politeness and precision. Conventional niceness and conformity are enough, it seems, to drive a person over the edge. A man who has suffered all his life from certain physical and intellectual liabilities is too weak to fend off these everyday affronts to dignity and truth. Like Dostoyevsky's underground man, Wilder is made to feel the stings of people's ordinariness. Yates does some of his best work when he stages the ludicrous and nauseating terms of the average person's stable life. People are either annoying purveyors of platitudes—like Wilder's wife, enthusing over the fresh pastries in a coffee shop or the fresh air on a country ride—or sadists like the nurse Charlie, with his genteel power plays. Usually the sadists are also pretentious: they torment you with showy speech or prestigious possessions. "Marjorie Wilder's Chocolates" are expensive, fussy, and ultimately deadly: in a late scene set in a California supermarket, the very sight of them causes Wilder to become violent, knock down a display, and take Pamela for a terrifying ride. This hysterical fit is the beginning of Wilder's final breakdown, which is to say his total inability to live among the sadists and simpletons.

In the final sections Yates also picks up another thread that has to do with tormentors. John Kennedy, Wilder's bête noire, comes to haunt him: in the last stages of his collapse, he imagines that he has killed the president; wandering the streets of Los Angeles, he attempts to turn himself in. John Wilder, like Fallon in "The B.A.R. Man," "attacks" a public figure who embodies privilege and power. But unlike Fallon, Wilder has gone mad in a way that wins him some sympathy. *Disturbing the Peace* accosts the reader with the very real external forces that drag Wilder down. Yates creates a world in which Wilder's paranoid fog and seething resentment are altogether comprehensible.

Yet ultimately the literary potency of a mad character is the crucial issue of the novel. Yes, Wilder is credible, but is his fragile being interesting enough to make Yates's book succeed? Has Yates drifted from the study of loneliness in his early stories into the exploration of mere pathology? Is Wilder a pathetic puppet or a man? Each reader will have to judge what John Wilder sees and endures: if everything is a mirror image of John's hopeless constitution, the novel is weakened; but if our argument is accepted, the reader will have seen the dreary and often cruel pull of everyday life and the way that the disturbed are overwhelmed by it.

A Funny Little School

Just as *Disturbing the Peace* charts the downfall of a little man, *A Good School* studies the breakup of "a funny little school."[10] Dorset Academy, a place that values individuality in its students, is the institutional equivalent of John Wilder: it lacks stature, dignity, basic survival skills. It fails during World War II, just at the time when America was gearing up for victory. It also has quantities of madness and anguish within its Disney-like "Cotswold" buildings in Connecticut.

Yates's story concentrates on all his familiar concerns—loss, class injury, ineptitude—but introduces the reader to an essentially upper-middle-class milieu that he has touched only in passing in *A Special Providence*. He treats this new territory with curious ambivalence: most of the time he forthrightly exposes the vulnerabilities of WASP preppies and their teachers. But at key moments, he gets close to the prep school mentality and shows respect for manners, civility, and the other staples of genteel education. Few novels about prep school life expose gentlemanly authority and show affection for it at the same time. Such ambivalence diminishes the satiric force of the book, making it a complex, nuanced treatment of class rather than an indictment or expose. Most of the "funny little" places and people in Yates are less than likable; but Dorset generates nostalgia and affection.

The protagonist, Bill Grove, paradoxically gains strength from being at a weak school: Yates has turned around the vision of *Disturbing the Peace* by showing how a troubled boy from a broken home can survive if he is left to develop in his own way. Dorset values individuality and honesty, two qualities in short supply in *Disturbing the Peace* or elsewhere in Yates; it is therefore quite possible that Bill can emerge from the awkwardness and mediocrity of his past life into a future of qualified success. As the son of a pretentious artist mother and a hard-working sales manager for General Electric, Bill begins as a nobody in the preppy world. By the end of the book he is the editor of the school newspaper and the roommate of the school's most intelligent student.

His tuition has been paid by a father who understands little of the prep school ethos; but one thing Grove does give to his son is a legacy of lyricism and emotion. The novel is framed by two portraits of Bill's father: first and last the father is remembered as a talented tenor, an amateur who gave up singing to earn a living. The "high, pure ribbon of sound" that Bill associates with his father is genuine and expressive (*AGS*, 177). As a heritage, put together by his adult son at the end of the book, it carries the father's qualities: tenderness, discipline, loneliness, self-sacrifice. His life of compromise and struggle is a more dignified version of the Dorset story: both are about the pain of giving up something valuable.

Bill's development is only a part of the story line. Each of the other characters tries to make Dorset a source of meaning, but most of them are depicted as they face various defeats and resign themselves to narrow futures. The boys and masters, as well as the women and girls, are part of a school that has never been "a real school" (*AGS,* 31). Based on a crazy millionairess's idea of freedom and gentility, Dorset is a cockeyed dream rather than a solid place. The boys are often the type that other schools wouldn't accept; the masters, although thoroughly competent, are most often compromised by life—disabled, unfocused, caught in a bad market. Football is intramural, sloppy, with too many touchdowns; dress regulations and architecture are all but laughable, inept copies of what better schools have. Altogether Dorset is another of Yates's yearning characters, a striving entity that isn't quite making it.

Yates finds weakness and injury everywhere: his narrative technique involves setting up various configurations of people whose connections with each other are damaged. Roommates, faculty couples, lovers, parents and children, all are depicted as they fail each other. By the end of the book, we know precisely why the school and its inmates have suffered defeat. Time after time we have watched "the sad silent display" of "hurt feelings."

But as Yates studies the losses, he also introduces what for him is always a triumph: the occasion when a person tries to put circumstances and self-interest aside, rise above suffering and numbness, and establish a true connection with another. While there are the usual number of short-circuited relationships in *A Good School,* there are many attempts to recover and repair: in this sense, the book is a quiet answer to Yates's own darkest pictures of isolation. The characters attempt to get back at their fates.

Bob "Pop" Driscoll, a Deerfield Academy graduate and a dedicated teacher of English, is shown struggling in the role of the school disciplinarian. His relationship with his lazy son and with other boys who are out of line is carefully developed. Young Bobby is a fat kid who would prefer to lounge around the living room than go to his dorm where he belongs: in a sense, he is "Pop" Driscoll's liability, a walking refutation of order and discipline. But Yates will not allow the conflict to be absolutely clear-cut; as it happens, Pop would like to get rid of Bobby so that he can make love to his wife on a Friday afternoon; he snaps at the boy because he is interfering with his pleasure.

Later in the novel, the self-absorbed person has a chance, which is almost always blocked in Yates, to offer some sign of affection. Bobby has been humiliated by a brutal group of dorm kids: their little prep school thing—masturbating a victim to prove he's a queer—is discovered by Pop; the scene shows the father talking kindly to his son and trying to get the boy to transcend the injury. Still later Pop is faced with a group of kids who have gone off on the eve of commencement and gotten drunk with some locals. He looks at the boys, most of them soon to be off to war, and forgets he's in charge of discipline. The perfect balance of the scene is achieved as Pop confronts Bill Grove, the dorm inspector who permitted his charges to go carousing: "he clapped the boy hard on the shoulder in what anyone would have said was affection" (*AGS*, 172). And then there is the brief episode when he takes the kids back: risking sentimentality, Yates has Pop breaking down in tears as he listens to their "tame little college boys' beer drinking song" (*AGS*, 172).

Yates's tack is to let the characters snatch something from their fragmented Dorset existences. The chemistry teacher Jack Draper, a polio victim, has been enduring his wife's affair with the French teacher, Jean-Paul La Prade. Yates traces this man's reactions to a condescending and often humiliating world. Draper observes the phony consideration of colleagues (and the salesmen in Brooks Brothers), Alice Draper's strange absences, and the small but definite indications of prejudice around him. Like John Wilder, he hates smarmy niceness and yearns to break through to a core of sincerity in his relationships.

Yates, however, refuses to let Draper be engulfed in disgust and despair. Instead he has his latest victim attempt suicide unsuccessfully and thereafter achieve a kind of unspectacular affirmation. Draper can't quite make his weak leg kick away a table in the chem lab so he can hang himself by his Brooks Brothers belt; he climbs down from his place of execution and resigns himself to going home and having a stiff bourbon "seated at the kitchen table of his own home, like a man" (*AGS*, 159). He also asserts the truth about himself, a protest against the world's genteel denials; when it comes time to leave Dorset and apply for another job, he refuses to leave out a description of his disability on a résumé that his wife is typing up. This firm stand against falsehood also seems to do something for his marriage. Readers will have to decide for themselves whether or not having Alice and Jack go off to the bedroom is too much. We would only venture the judgment that Yates can very easily lapse into corniness in his treatment of sex: in everything after *Revolutionary Road* and *Eleven Kinds of Loneliness,* there are characters, especially males, who rhapsodize about passion and ruin the subtle distancing in relationships that makes Yates an unusual kind of realist.

Other people in *A Good School* are given nuanced portrayals: Yates lets us see their despair mixed with their desire to get back at the school and the society that renders them powerless. Several boys, including Bill, endure the battering of the American class system. Lothar Brundels, son of the school chef, tells how it feels to have a father like Louie Brundels, a little man who is introduced wearing a chef's hat at the Thanksgiving dinner for parents. He and Bill Grove, writers for the *Dorset Chronicle,* also discuss clothes and what's "proletarian." It turns out that he and Bill both look prole in their big-shouldered suits and pleated pants.

The preppy/prole conflict permeates the novel. Like Yates himself, Bill is anxious to escape the stigma of the lower class and is at the same time contemptuous of fanciness and phony status displays. (Be it noted that Yates preserved the preppy style—the oxford cloth button-down shirts, the tweed jackets, the old-fashioned courteous manner— throughout his life.) Bill's father visits Dorset just at the time when the topic of class is most pressing: Bill and Lothar are hurt, angry, and anxious about their poor image, but Grove's father comes forward with a kind of grace and understatement that dispels the injuries. The other boys could never say that, in his three-piece suit and watch chain (he never quite noticed that people had switched to wrist watches), Grove was "decidedly middle class" (*AGS,* 79). For once an out-of-step character carries some dignity.

But Bill, an unprepossessing outsider at Dorset, has trouble making his mark. The brutish razzing that Bobby Driscoll endured was also his fate in his first year at school; his scholarship has been very poor; his French teacher has labeled him as a boy with psychological problems. Yates's attitude toward this last mark of woe fits perfectly with his general contempt for psychology: in Bill's world "any word beginning with 'psych' had come to frighten him. All such words spoke of a darkness beyond hope" (*AGS,* 81). And if we recall the nail biters and candy eaters and slick operators among the shrinks in Yates's works, we can also infer that "psych" is not classy: it's part of a humiliating culture of vulnerability. Yates the observer of weak people prefers not to join the "psych" types and instead concentrates on the social sphere. If this is denial and repression, it surely does not come off as such when we observe Yates's attention to weakness and injury.

A Good School locates people's psychological problems in the competitive arena of work and socializing, not in the depths of the subconscious. The slips in the book are not Freudian but banana peel in type; they reveal clumsiness and faulty playing rather than casebook pathology. As a school that accepts problem boys and values individuality, Dorset is a showcase for adolescent mistakes. Typical of Yates are the scenes in which boys foil themselves. Bucky Ward, a wry campus character who wants to be Bill Grove's pal, destroys their relationship by nonstop chit-chat with a boy who needs to establish his separateness. Bucky is great at witty banter, but as he muses on life and meaning and love, he becomes another wearisome Yates talker. Hoping to build up his own reputation, Bill feels uneasy about being close with such a character. Others, including the superintelligent Hugh Britt, feel uneasy about being close to Bill. The chain of vulnerability extends from one end of the school to the other, including discerning masters who feel uneasy about the pathetic little school and students who feel uncomfortable with less well favored classmates.

In an especially sharp scene, Bucky leads Bill to a quiet spot beside a brook in order to talk about a problem. It seems that Bill has secured a new roommate, and Bucky wants an explanation. But as they start to talk, Bill notices that Larry Gaines, the school golden boy, and Edith Stone, a popular faculty child, are trysting. The ludicrousness of the two couples' meeting (the "shy greetings—'Hi'; 'Hi' ") in a romantic spot—one, quite appropriately; the other, unwittingly and awkwardly—stresses Bill's mistake about chumming with Bucky and of course his embarrassment about sex (*AGS*, 132). Bill and Bucky had become fast friends and had once laughed for hours like lovers; but this unintentional closeness is something that Bill must destroy in the interest of breaking out of his isolation; to be popular and wholesome in the eyes of brainy Hugh Britt, Bill has to distance himself from a pal: like others in the Yates gallery of lonely people, he must endure separation in order not to be separated from the group. He is a late version of the anxious recruits in "Jody Rolled the Bones," the difference being that this time the sacrifice is worth it. Bill comes out ahead.

At crucial points in the narrative, the reader does not know whether to weep or laugh at the social mishaps. Small breakups and break-downs—collapsed friendships and shattered nerves—make for the book's episode-to-episode structure; they neatly foreshadow the end of Dorset Academy. Terry Flynn, a good-looking athlete who cannot read well, is portrayed as a sad, silly case trying to keep up with glamorous Jim Pomeroy. This, of course, is a variation of the Grove/Ward conflict—indeed, one of Yates's fundamental lessons about the brutality of social life at school, or in the suburbs with Frank Wheeler and his less well endowed neighbor Shep Campbell.

It all comes down to embarrassment about one person's weaknesses. An awkward series of scenes with the two boys, including the episode when Pomeroy wants to tell Flynn that they are finished as roommates, crackles with misery and comedy. Such scenes are defining moments for many Dorset boys, times when they either assert power or submit to it. First, Flynn comes back to school and decorates their room with flouncy yellow curtains and eight framed pictures of New England; Pomeroy squirms, but finally feels all right when several guys compliment the changes. But soon after, Yates shows Pomeroy getting wise to the academic and emotional weaknesses of Flynn and mercilessly picking a fight in order to get rid of him. We watch Terry Flynn sobbing and lashing out at the provoking Pomeroy; and once again, Brooks Brothers, a status symbol and preppy establishment across the generations, is mentioned as we see Terry shaking in his best tweed jacket. It goes without saying that the other two references to the store have also highlighted Jack Draper, the man with the Brooks Brothers belt.

Yates's mixture of sardonic humor and pathos engulfs other awkward people. Most of the time they are fairly likable victims who suffer because they miscalculate society's responses: the highly intellectual and pretentious John Haskell, who cracks up and runs away from school; the eccentric Pierre Van Loon, who can't help socializing with the kitchen help and the local blue-collar people and who likes to talk about boring science fiction stories; "little Dave Hutchins," who can't assert authority, even though he is president of the student council; Alice Draper, who can't help begging and whining and pleading for attention from the sexy French teacher La Prade; and Bill Grove himself, who is surrounded by an aura of incompetence and unwholesomeness until his shining senior year as editor of the *Dorset Chronicle* (*AGS*, 163). Even the all-round types like Larry Gaines, Hugh Britt, and Pop Driscoll are diminished or destroyed.

The reader, of course, must decide whether they are treated like fish in a barrel, the easy prey of a marksman with an eye for weakness, or whether they are complex people who have a chance at happiness before they are killed off or crushed. The latter interpretation, it seems, is confirmed only to a point: even Yates's best people are bedeviled by the culture of failure at the "funny little school." They are marked for extinction or misery or mediocrity. After enjoying an hour or two of perfect love with young Edith Stone, Larry goes off on a merchant ship, only to die in a freakish explosion at sea. Pop Driscoll, who seemed like a pillar of strength, breaks down. Britt is swallowed up by a nondescript career in the midwest. Altogether, Bill seems like the sturdiest survivor: having learned his craft—and having made every possible mistake at Dorset—he is prepared to face the world with guarded hope.

Chapter 5

Liars in Love and the Lowered Expectations of the 1970s

Richard Yates published only two collections of stories, *Eleven Kinds of Loneliness* and *Liars in Love*; they differ in subject, in technique, and in Yates's closeness to his characters.[1] The stories in *Liars in Love* are complicated, often having many fully sketched-out characters involved in actions that take months or years, and the stories themselves are twice the length of those in *Eleven Kinds of Loneliness*. The market for slick fiction, specifically that market paying real money for short stories, dried up between the early 1950s, when Yates had virtually completed the stories in *Eleven Kinds of Loneliness,* and the late 1970s, when he published *Liars in Love*. Although *Eleven Kinds of Loneliness* was published in 1962, at the peak of Yates's critical reputation, its oldest stories had been drafted as far back as the late 1940s, when the apprentice Yates was learning how to write stories that would at once satisfy his standards and find a home in popular magazines. By the late 1970s, though, Yates was writing stories without much thought as to which magazine might publish them; most of *Liars in Love* was never published in periodical form.

For better or worse, *Eleven Kinds of Loneliness* was made up of *short stories,* which is to say they were clearly fictional constructs crafted to embody particular types. This attention to craft would be only natural during a period when Yates was doggedly teaching himself how to construct fiction. But for all his characters's virtues, some of them seem less than fully three-dimensional. J. D. Salinger, who was also publishing his apprentice fiction in the slick magazine market of the late 1940s (with rather more success than Yates), later described his fictional alter ego, Buddy Glass, submitting a late 1940s short story for his brother's criticism: Seymour Glass comments on the falseness of the story's conventional opening ("Henshaw woke up that morning with a splitting head"), a falseness that caused him to lose his faith in the existence of all such fictional Henshaws.[2] And some stories in *Eleven Kinds of Loneliness* are peopled by Henshaws, conveniently crafted mouthpieces serving as their story's vehicles—Walter Henderson, for example, might be so described.

Where *Eleven Kinds of Loneliness*'s heartaches include the pain of children growing up in single-parent homes—a pain Yates had felt deeply and never accepted, much less forgot about—*Liars in Love*'s principal subject is the survivors of such homes. While Yates was writing *Eleven Kinds of Loneliness,* that subject had haunted him; of all the pains he had witnessed or felt, the pain of being a child of divorce had marked his psyche the deepest. But one event had changed his life between his two collections of short fiction, expanding his perspective on that pain: in 1959, when he had already long since written almost all of *Eleven Kinds of Loneliness,* his marriage broke up, making him now not only a child of divorce, but a divorced adult inflicting on his two young daughters that very pain he had felt so severely himself.[3]

"Richard Yates is the author of a forthcoming collection of short stories entitled *Broken Homes,*" a blurb announced shortly before the publication of the hastily retitled *Liars in Love.*[4] Yates had been thinking of the collection as stories about broken homes during much of its composition. On the back of a typescript page in "Saying Goodbye to Sally" he penciled a note: "Dedication in *Broken Homes:* To My Daughters," which is in fact the dedication to *Liars in Love.* The title *Broken Homes* had been changed from his original working title, *Five Kinds of Dismay,* a labored reworking of his first collection's title. The collection eventually contained seven stories, not five, but Yates evidently considered even five stories enough to warrant collecting—these stories were very long. His agent allowed for the unusual length of these fictions, stretching the genre's borders by pitching *Five Kinds of Dismay* as "a new book made up of five short stories/novellas."[5]

Vestiges of later novels are buried in these stories (compare the plot line and theme of the story "A Natural Girl" to the 1984 novel *Young Hearts Crying.*) Composing the *Liars in Love* stories as possible novels instead of slick magazine fictions would in itself make them more discursive, but Yates's vision of what he wanted his fiction to do also became increasingly complex. More and more, he needed to explore in depth and at length minuscule matters that other authors might have at some point considered settled issues—indeed, reexamining such issues became a Yates earmark, as his characters question their own motives for making choices that often seem self-explanatory. Yates's aversion to filling the needs of potential publishers—a perverse if subconscious possibility—may have also affected the length of his later work, in that in

Yates's last few decades, his short stories grew too long, generally, to be placed in magazines, while his novels increasingly grew slighter and slighter, shrinking to the point where their commercial viability almost vanished. He certainly could have made his work more easily publishable if he had written in each genre at the more normative length of his first short stories and novels.

Perhaps the second change of the collection's title, from *Broken Homes* to *Liars in Love,* was intended to avoid the charge of deliberate and self-indulgent melancholy, a charge that followed him throughout his career. (He would protest indignantly that his work had its spots of merriment and good humor, and it did, but not enough to affect the overall gloomy tone.) *Liars in Love* is a wittier title, certainly, but the starkness of *Broken Homes* is truer to the collection's tone and imagery.

The concept of "home" reverberates throughout Yates's work. That word recurs over and over in the collection's final story, "Saying Goodbye to Sally," and is crucial to the story "Regards at Home." In general, "home" is one of the central lies that Yates can't resist pointing out—the word affords his weak characters a measure of false solace, allowing them to justify all sorts of disastrous choices in the name of an abstraction whose main quality, permanence, rarely proves true. In a sense, the rhetoric of *Broken Homes* parallels that of *Liars in Love;* both titles yoke an almost holy abstraction, "Home" and "Love," to the profane reality of impermanence and untruth.

The theme of *Liars in Love* is self-deception. Yates's more complex characters know they are deceiving themselves, and feel guilty about lying, and wonder why they tell lies to themselves. The question of their identities inevitably arises: are they so afraid of the truth about themselves, Yates's characters wonder, that they prefer to live shrouded in self-deceit?

The stories in *Liars in Love* are discussed here in roughly the order that they draw closer and closer to Richard Yates's own life story. The first story under discussion, "A Compassionate Leave," is about a character whose biography differs from Yates's in small but meaningful ways. The failure to bond with another person is the subject of the next story under discussion, "A Natural Girl," which also charts out the precise biographical links between Yates and his protagonists in *Liars in Love.* "Saying Goodbye to Sally," "Trying Out for the Race," and "Liars in Love" examine a variety of sexual roles, all of which prove inadequate in Yates, and "Regards at Home" and "Oh, Joseph, I'm So Tired" are all but explicitly autobiographical works, drawing little or no distinction between Yates's artistic concerns and his personal ones, and lead into a discussion of his explicitly autobiographical second novel, *A Special Providence.*

A Life Suspended

Like virtually all of Richard Yates's protagonists, Paul Colby in "A Compassionate Leave" is scarred by his broken home. When Colby was 11 years old, his English mother divorced his American father, snatched his sister, and returned to London, leaving Colby to be raised by his father. Although most of "A Compassionate Leave" is set when Colby is 19 and serving in the U.S. Army occupying Europe soon after World War II, his parents' divorce propels the story's plot. Private Colby requests "a compassionate leave" to visit his estranged English half-family and, while he waits for his request to be processed, he reflects on the crucial moment when the dissolution of his family "amounted to an almost unendurable loss."[6]

At first, however, he is falsely made to seem primarily concerned with another, far more trivial, type of loss. He appears to suffer from nothing more profound than a malady common to gawky 19-year-olds: an excess of virginity. His inept attempts to divest himself of that burden take up most of the narrative of "A Compassionate Leave," but the true and underlying issue, it develops, concerns the trauma of his parents' divorce.

The bare plot of "A Compassionate Leave" is potentially comical: the awkward Colby stumbles through a continent giddy with relief at the war's end, which every soldier and civilian is celebrating as orgiastically as possible. But "A Compassionate Leave" is far from comical. This tale, as Yates tells it, is grim, and Paul Colby, far from a figure of fun, is a genuinely wretched figure whose virginity weighs far more heavily on him than on other teenagers. To Colby, it is the last remaining link to his childhood, which he nurtures despite every conscious move he makes to eradicate it. Though now a weary veteran, Colby is no adult. His adult self—the outward and visible self—is dislocated in the miasma of childish fantasies and lies he tells himself.

As long as he remains a virgin he can remain, in some strict technical sense, a child, and can therefore entertain fantasies of seeing his parents reconciled, his lost sister found, his childhood regained. In a literal sense, by seeking to visit his mother and sister, he is reconciling his family. Losing his virginity will signify that he has become an adult who must accept the rift between his parents as a permanent one.

Throughout "A Compassionate Leave," Colby feels inadequate and vaguely guilty, although he can never articulate quite what he has done or failed to do. Confused and guilt-ridden over his inadequacy in keeping his parents together, he recapitulates that inadequacy in his sexuality, and the world around him seems to join in his vague sense of guilt.

"A Compassionate Leave" is, for Yates, unusual in structure, in that it begins with a long expository section describing the general setting and atmosphere of a whole army division without even mentioning Yates's eventual protagonist. The luckless 57th Division has been assigned to camp out in the boondocks of rural France, far from Paris and Berlin, where postwar celebrations are being enjoyed by luckier GIs. "Many of them wondered if this was their punishment for having been indifferent soldiers," Yates writes (*LIL*, 143). Like any other ex-soldier, Yates knew perfectly well how little merit influences which assignments army divisions draw. But guilt over being mediocre soldiers makes Yates's sad sacks feel that they somehow deserve this miserable assignment. Like the child of divorce he is, Colby wonders what he might have done to cause his unhappy state, and how he might have prevented it. He entertains any explanation, however contrary to logic, that blames his own insignificant actions.

While Yates recognizes the pointless masochism of dwelling on luck, good or bad, the hapless soldiers of the 57th Division, caught in luck's fist, don't share that rational point of view. A soldier named Phelps suggests that the division's bad luck is somehow good for them: "We got fresh air, we got shelter, we got food, we got discipline," Phelps argues. "This is a man's life" (*LIL*, 145). The others, including Paul Colby, jeer at Phelps, but Colby secretly sympathizes with the ridiculed soldier's philosophy: while the other soldiers wholeheartedly deride Phelps's sexless and joyless paradise, Colby takes comfort in the unchallenging quality Phelps describes. Ironically, what he likes most about it is that it is not a man's life, it is a boy's, and that's just fine with him. Colby, "too, had come to like the simplicity, the order, and the idleness of life in these tents in the grass. There was nothing to prove here" (*LIL*, 146).

Colby feels safe in the postwar Army precisely because it is so limiting. In the army he can avoid, or at least postpone, becoming a man. Like Walter Henderson, he enjoys wielding no power over his own life. Paul Colby is focused purely on the outward show he's giving—on his performance, in Goffman's sense of the term—and he does so passable a performance as an adult, as a soldier, as a regular guy (secretly admiring Phelps's point of view, privately feeling relief at having his choices made for him) that he manages to fool himself into thinking he's doing okay.

While Colby's leave is pending, the story's action is likewise suspended. The scene shifts to Paris, where Colby has a three-day pass. He makes the trip "on a morning bright with promise" of ending his virginal status, accompanied by another young private named George Mueller (*LIL,* 154). Although their friendship is introduced in terms of their similarities, Mueller's function in the story is not to recapitulate Colby's but to contrast with it.

They confess their virginity to each other, forming a private bond, but some important distinctions between these two virgins emerge. Mueller's descriptions of his inept attempts to couple with a woman are genuinely comical and utterly unambiguous in conveying Mueller's devotion to achieving his goal. Colby cannot confess equally frank details, because they would show how he, and not circumstances or bad luck or his inexperience, had caused him to remain a virgin.

In Paris, Mueller's sincere efforts pay off and highlight Colby's complicity in his seeming lack of luck. Alone in Paris, where he might yet contrive to hook up with a prostitute, Colby instead squanders all his money on cheap wine, sitting in cafés, finding "various ways to compose himself at different tables, and soon he began to wonder how he must look to casual observers" (*LIL,* 160). He evaluates his performance generously while he can still afford wine, concluding "that he probably looked like a sensitive young man," but when the wine and all his money have vanished, he soberly realizes that "he couldn't afford even the most raucous of middle-aged whores now, and he knew he had probably arranged in his secret heart for this to be so" (*LIL,* 160–61).

After Mueller has served to set Colby's sexual agenda in high relief, Colby meets another teenager with whom he contrasts even more sharply. Granted his compassionate leave, Colby goes to London to visit his estranged younger sister, whose maturity and sexual sophistication far outstrip his. The relationship between the Colby siblings is charged with an odd sexual tension. Colby's every action with women in the story—several of whom he might easily have taken to bed—stressed his sexual incompetence, but now with his own sister, whom he cannot take to bed, his air is confident and jaunty. Like Frank Wheeler with his terrifically sexy walk, Colby is conscious of his body language: "trying in every stride to perfect what he hoped would be a devil-may-care kind of walk," he meets his sister, Marcia, and literally sweeps her off her feet, "and he brought it off well, probably from his self-tutelage in the devil-may-care walk" (*LIL,* 164–65). Colby "kept congratulating himself on how well he was doing"—with his own sister!—and "couldn't find anything the matter with his performance" (*LIL,* 165).

His performance, sexual and otherwise, remains an issue when his attention turns to his sister's physical appearance: "He had been so concerned with himself that he didn't realize until now, offering a light for her cigarette, what a pretty girl she was. And it wasn't only in the face; she was nice all the way down" (*LIL,* 166). She tells him of her various boyfriends, among whom she is choosing a husband. While her older brother is paralyzed at the thought of entering an adult relationship, she is sophisticated, claiming that falling in love is merely a matter of deciding who to do it with. To Paul Colby, love and sex and other adult things simply and mysteriously happen to people able to exert control over events, which rules him out.

The next night, Paul visits his sister's apartment, where her older roommate inadvertently reveals that Marcia perceives correctly Paul's virginity, and that she pities him for it. Embarrassed, Marcia apologizes and commiserates with Paul but soon brings up again the dread subject of his virginity. Another apology quickly follows, but he has been humiliated irretrievably. With consummate falseness, she hugs him good-bye, crying dramatically, "Oh, my brother" (*LIL,* 172). Just before they part she assures him, "I know you'll be all right. We'll both be all right. It's awfully important to believe that" (*LIL,* 172).

Since she can't empathize with her brother for more than a moment at a stretch, and since he seems permanently impaired, it's doubtful that they will ever be all right, either together or apart. This ironic parting benediction echoes all through *Liars in Love,* where characters use that signature phrase to claim, hollowly, a kind of triumph in disaster. "A Compassionate Leave" ends as Paul abandons plans to see his mother, which is to say he relinquishes his childhood fantasy about finding a home.

There Is No Why

Like Paul Colby's sister, leaving him with the lie that they "will be all right," the title character in "A Natural Girl" listens to her husband reassuring her, with more hope than confidence, that their troubled marriage will survive: "Let me tell you something," David Clark says to his wife, Susan, just before the climax of the story, "We'll be all right" (*LIL,* 55).

"A Natural Girl" turns on a dime at that point, as Susan tells him something: "No, we won't." He is stunned, but she goes on: "I said no we won't. We haven't been all right for a long time and we aren't all right now and it isn't going to get any better."

The self-assurance with which Susan conducts her life is the subject of "A Natural Girl," but the emptiness of that autonomy is the story's theme. Yates exposes Susan's cool mysterious nature, initially so admirable and attractive, as selfish and cruel. He does this largely through juxtaposition and repetition, making her considered responses, when seen often enough, seem irrationally self-protective. He explores the nature of an exotic, strangely unknowable specimen of American womanhood. Susan's resistance to intimacy is what at first attracts David Clark: he admires her spunk, which he himself lacks. But when she turns on him, those very traits cause him great pain.

Susan's chemistry doesn't mix badly only with David's. She brings her mixture of aloofness and autonomy to every intimate male relationship she has, starting with her father, who acts as David Clark's foil through the story. "A Natural Girl" explains the relationship Susan has with these two men: in the opening scene, Susan rejects her father for no apparent reason and takes comfort in the arms of her boyfriend, David Clark, who seems to give her the love she requires. She and David marry, have a daughter, and seem to fulfill each other, which only makes more mysterious the odd opening scene of Susan dismissing her father in heartless and unfeeling terms. Had Susan's father, before the story began, done something unspeakable to her? What might have happened between them? These questions get resolved when she suddenly and unilaterally ends her marriage to David. Now, because Susan chooses the same tone of voice and, without realizing it, chooses to end her marriage with the exact words she had chosen to end her relationship with her father, it becomes clear that the mystery, as the title implies, lies not in the relationships but in Susan's nature.

The strangeness of the other sex is a central problem in "A Natural Girl." Susan's outward loveliness is appreciated by both David Clark and Dr. Edward Andrews, but it is her inner nature that draws both men to her. David Clark and Dr. Andrews are drawn by the composure and self-assurance that later come to devastate them. Her father fondly remembers her utter independence as a child, a self-possession that bordered on defiance, which made her stand out from the crowd of her six sisters.

Susan challenges her father, and men in general, to understand her, but she holds something vital of herself back from them, frustrating their knowledge of her. The story's title implies that this quality is by no means willful on Susan's part, but is part and parcel of her nature. Like the scorpion in Orson Welles's *Mr. Arkadin,* who justifies his murderous and ultimately suicidal impulse with the remark, "It is my character, and there is no logic in character," Susan refuses to be held accountable for her self-centered acts. Just before she dashes David Clark's illusion of contentment, he tells her that "Sometimes it's hard to tell what you're thinking. It always has been." Instead of taking this observation as a chance to examine her insularity, she remarks, "I suppose that's something I can't help, isn't it?" (*LIL,* 54). Then, autonomy intact, she breaks the news to him: she has decided that their marriage is over.

Most of "A Natural Girl" is told from the point of view of David Clark, but there are frequent shifts in points of view: the beginning and ending sections are told from the father's perspective, and, for a few paragraphs, from the perspective of the main character herself. As he did in *Revolutionary Road* with April Wheeler, Yates gives us privileged glimpses into the mind of his main female character but strategically withholds her perspective at precisely the moments the reader most needs them. This withholding of key information makes Susan Andrews Clark seem more inscrutable than she would have seemed if Yates had omitted her point of view entirely. This way, the reader, like Susan's father and her husband, has the illusion of intimacy with her.

Near the end of the story, when the point of view has shifted back to Dr. Andrews's perspective, he thinks, "Girls. Would they always drive you crazy? Would their smiles of rejection always drop you into despair and their smiles of welcome lead you only into new, worse, more terrible ways of breaking your heart? . . . Oh, dear Christ," Andrews despairs, echoing Freud's despairing *What do women want?* "how in the whole of a lifetime could anybody understand girls?" (*LIL,* 60–61).

The quality that attracts men and women is the very quality that eventually drives them apart: their strangeness to each other. Initially, Yates is saying, this strangeness seems exotic and enticing, but sooner or later it becomes off-putting. Men and women hope eventually to understand each other, and rise to the challenge of doing so, but finally come to see the daunting wall between them as insurmountable.

The concept of nature, at first blush, has a positive connotation. The very title "A Natural Girl" implies that Susan will be spontaneous and unaffected, which she is. But nature is no more kind than it is unkind, and the natural traits that attracted David when she broke with her father now hurt and puzzle him. But he is too romantic for his own good, too willing to trust nature to treat him kindly.

Like all romantics, he should have been able to see his disaster coming but chooses not to. Susan's emotions are as changeable as the weather, and from the first David Clark knows not to rely on her for constancy or logic. When her broken-hearted father, seeking to summon up some shred of dignity after his best-loved daughter flatly tells him she no longer loves him, says, "All right, you don't love me. But tell me this much, dear. Tell me why," she answers him, "There is no why. There's no more why to not loving than there is to loving. I think most intelligent people understand that" (*LIL*, 37–38). David comforts her when she comes to him, distressed by this confrontation, reassuring her that if she writes her father a letter, then she'll "be able to put the whole thing behind you. That's what people do, haven't you noticed? They put things behind them." This advice will backfire—when Susan breaks with him, he will be unable to put it behind him, and his father-in-law will then wonder what "the poor son of a bitch [was] going to do with the rest of his life"—but worst of all is David's failure to see that Susan is, even in this crisis, not looking to him for advice, support, or comfort (*LIL*, 58). Her autonomy disturbs him because he assumes that Susan needs emotional support the same way he does. So he forces it on her, but "she withdrew from him to grieve in solitude, in another room, and the silence went on too long for his liking" (*LIL*, 43).

His liking or disliking is a matter of supreme indifference to her—whichever one it is, she sees it only as unsolicited and obtrusive—while David is terribly needful of her emotional support. David Clark has the Yatesian trait of turning large and small issues over in his mind, never quite sure if he has enough information to make a decision, never self-confident enough to accept the decision he just made, and he brings these doubts to his young bride, who has no sympathy for his vacillating nature: his constantly shifting career goals—from academic to political speechwriter back to academic again—disturb him, but Susan is more annoyed by his questioning something as "natural" as his own inconsistency: "These years away from the classroom, he explained, had simply been a mistake—not a bad or costly mistake, perhaps even one he could ultimately find profit in—but a mistake nonetheless. He was a school man. He had always been a school man, and would probably always be." Characteristically undermining a strong assertion with a sudden expression of doubt, Yates concludes by backtracking: "'Unless,' he said, looking suddenly shy, 'unless you think of all this as kind of—going backwards, or something' " (*LIL*, 54).

Ignoring her husband's point, Susan instead wonders out loud, "Why would I think that?" (*LIL*, 54). Doubting her own decisions is as alien to her nature as it is habitual to his. Soon, after she announces she is leaving him, he can't accept the news. He summarizes the significance of her announcement:

"My God, you really mean this, don't you. I've really lost you, haven't I?
You don't—love me anymore."
   "That's right," she said. "Exactly. I don't love you anymore."
   "Well, but for Christ's sake, Susan, why? Can you tell me why?"

The astute reader will, at this point, remember her response to her
father's identical question at the other end of the story, but David either
has no memory or else he is falling into the rhetorical trap she has set:
"'There is no why,' she [repeats]. 'There's no more why to not loving
than there is to loving. Isn't that something most intelligent people
understand?' " (LIL, 55-6).
   Written shortly after Yates's second divorce in 1975, "A Natural Girl"
originally contained some of the frankest autobiographical passages in
his work. Although this material was deleted from the final published
manuscript, the early drafts show his sense of awareness that he could
not easily write about his childhood traumas: "I must've had the most
fucked-up childhood in American History," David confesses to Susan in
this early draft. "I've told you a lot about my parents and all that . . . but
I've always held back. I've never gotten down to the pain of it. And the
worst part, you see, the neurotic part, is that I've never really faced the
pain of it myself. I've been hiding and pretending, all my life" (BU-Y).
   Profoundly hostile to psychotherapy, Yates could be set off on a tirade
when certain conversational buttons were pushed, and Freudian jargon
was a big red button for him. In this passage, David Clark, whose views
Yates otherwise shared, spouts psychiatry's most basic tenet, which may
well explain why this passage was cut before publication. There is a
tremendous gap between David's "I must've had the most fucked-up
childhood in American History" and Yates's crisp summation to an
interviewer, "I had an OK childhood" (Venant).
   A few sentences after this omitted passage, there appears in the early
draft of "A Natural Girl" another passage Yates also deleted: "And then
this whole thing of my admiration for Frank Brady. Trying to please
him, putting myself in a servile position with him every day—kissing
his ass everyday, if you like—well, Jesus, do you see what that suggests?
Do you see what all that really comes down to? The search for a father.
Pure and simple" (BU-Y).
   The search for a father does creep subtly but unquestionably into
Yates's other writing ("Oh, Joseph, I'm So Tired" and A Special Providence
most prominently) but never so nakedly as in this passage. Yates may
have felt that such passages were criticizing the fiction rather than
extending it and so rejected them, yet they touch on issues that kept

Yates's fiction circling around the same topics for years without ever resolving them. Like his characters who return helplessly to question decisions they have made, Yates returns to reexamine topics he has dealt with, well and sometimes definitively, before.

"A Natural Girl" seems a sketch toward the novel *Young Hearts Crying,* which would be his next publication after *Liars in Love.* Both this story and that novel concern the failure of an academic in the early 1970s to achieve in his second marriage the satisfaction that eluded him in his first. A virtually identical scene, for example, appears in both works: a middle-aged academic is humiliated by his lack of stamina when his young wife takes him bicycling. The issue of Vietnam becomes central to both: here this burning question is one that David Clark feels passionately about, only to lose that passion suddenly. Rather than taking a political position, which he rarely did, Yates used the political issue to illustrate David's vacillation on major as well as minor topics; Yates's own politics play a very small part in his work.

Much of "A Natural Girl" can be traced directly to Yates's second marriage: like David Clark, he married a midwestern student of his in the late 1960s, had a daughter with her, and the marriage foundered in the mid-1970s. In fact, every story in *Liars in Love* contains a character whose life story resembles that of Richard Yates, either closely or very closely. In the stories, ranging from the early 1930s to the mid-1970s, there is always some male figure who is precisely Yates's age at just that moment:

Story	Name of character	year story is set	age of Yates and character in that year
"Oh, Joseph . . ."	Billy Grove	1933	7
"A Natural Girl"	David Clark	1973	47
"Trying Out for the Race"	Russell Towers	1935	9
"Liars in Love"	Warren Mathews	1953	27
"A Compassionate Leave"	Paul Colby	1945	19
"Regards at Home"	Bill Grove	1949	23
"Saying Goodbye to Sally"	Jack Fields	1962	36

More than merely chronologically similar, these characters are doing the same things Yates was doing in those years. Like Paul Colby, for example, Yates was serving in the infantry in 1945; like David Clark, he was a disillusioned former speechwriter who tries his hand at academe in the late 1960s; and like Jack Fields, he was a Hollywood scriptwriter in 1962.

Writing about Writers

"Writers who write about writers," Yates acknowledged in the 1961 story "Builders," "can easily bring on the worst kind of literary miscarriage," but Yates managed to avoid this miscarriage while still writing intensely about his own life (*11K*, 191). Mostly he carried it off by writing about his nonwriting life: his experience as a child, for example, or as an alcoholic, or as an academic, or as a soldier contributed to his fiction as much as his primary job as a writer. "Saying Goodbye to Sally" not only violates his warning against writing about writers, however, it takes it one step further: it is a story about a writer who examines his literary roots.

Richard Yates was a self-educated student of the craft of writing, and his own tastes largely determined the course of his self-chosen curriculum. F. Scott Fitzgerald topped the list of "some very good masters" Yates wrote about fondly in a *New York Times Book Review* article of that name, and in "Saying Goodbye to Sally" Yates explicitly acknowledges Fitzgerald's importance in his fiction, a rarity for the unliterary, though hardly unlearned, Yates ("Masters"). Fitzgerald was an autodidact, too, despite three years at Princeton, and Yates looked to him for a guide in how to live and how to write. Their lives followed similar patterns, the most notable exception being a large one: Fitzgerald enjoyed great early success before spending his last decade in a Yatesian financial and literary struggle. Both writers' families had moved constantly, and both writers, even when grown, continued to change their addresses every few months. Both suffered from tuberculosis and bouts of alcoholism, and the combination of poverty and alcohol induced nervous breakdowns in both writers, wrenching experiences that they incorporated into their work, Fitzgerald in *The Crack-up*, Yates in *Disturbing the Peace* and *Young Hearts Crying*.

Most to the point here, Fitzgerald found a safety valve for his financial pressures in Hollywood, where in the late 1930s he was paid generously to produce very little, if his productiveness can be measured by the screenplays that made it to the screen.[7] Yates repeated Fitzgerald's Hollywood pilgrimage a quarter-century afterward, eagerly grasping at lucrative scriptwriting work whether or not he found the work artistically satisfying. Like Fitzgerald's screenwriting, what little of Yates's that ended up on the screen was undistinguished, and like Fitzgerald, he squirreled away a few kernels of truth from the experience and turned them into fiction sporadically. "Saying Goodbye to Sally" is Yates's only work set almost entirely in Hollywood, and it is the only one so haunted by a literary forebear.

Yates's protagonist is a 36-year-old fiction writer named Jack Fields, whose fiction, like Yates's at the age of 36, is critically praised but not widely read. Living a squalid, unproductive life on the East Coast, slipping into the early stages of alcoholism, Fields jumps at the chance to write the screenplay to a novel he had admired. (Yates went to Hollywood in the spring of 1962 to write a screenplay of William Styron's *Lie Down in Darkness*.) When the scriptwriting offer rescues him from his financial, emotional, and creative torpor, Fields remembers that Fitzgerald had been rescued in that way, and consciously patterns his California stay on Fitzgerald's.

In Los Angeles, Fields meets a woman with whom he builds a relationship modeled on Fitzgerald's with Sheilah Graham, who after Fitzgerald's death described their love affair in several tawdry books, most notoriously *Beloved Infidel*. In that book, Graham—like Fields's girlfriend, Sally Baldwin—helps her lover adapt to California, encourages him to socialize, and worries about his commitment to her. Having invested a lot of emotion and energy, she wonders if he will be willing to repay that investment once he straightens out his finances, overcomes his drinking problem, and rehabilitates his writing career. In other words, Sheilah and Sally have to ask themselves if this is love or just a fling, and neither woman likes the answer she gets.

In their permanently impermanent lives, Fields and Fitzgerald surely knew that California was not a place for them to flourish but a place for them to lick their wounds. So their sense of gratitude toward their California mistresses was accompanied by a powerful sense of guilt. Both had roots on the East Coast, where their best writing had been done and where the shards of their shattered marriages were strewn; they had open contempt for California's brand of culture, for the industry they worked in, and for the work they did. Both men treated Los Angeles as criminals treat a hideout and were eager to leave it as soon as they patched themselves up. Yet they had to hide this eagerness from their new lovers.

Fields also feels he must hide his admiration for Fitzgerald. He finds it tinged with hero worship, and he realizes how any parallels necessarily aggrandize him. Curiously, Yates restrains himself from making certain parallels more explicit: Graham, for example, was mightily ashamed of the lower-class origins she felt her birth name, Lily Shields, betrayed. Yates merely mentions in passing that Sally Baldwin, born with the equally clumsy name of "Sally Munk," was grateful that a previous marriage had left her with a more elegant name, just as Graham's brief marriage entitled her to use her ex-husband's name.[8] Yates also alludes to Fitzgerald's published notebooks when he has Sally confess that she can't bear children. Fitzgerald's notebooks contain the couplet

Every California girl has lost at least one ovary,
And none of them has read *Madame Bovary*[9]

which Yates had almost certainly read, since he has Fields passing along Fitzgerald's quip *"Honi Soit Qui Malibu,"* a mangled form of the aphorism *"honi soit qui mal y pense"* that Fitzgerald had written in the notebooks (Fitzgerald, 57). Yates raises a metafictional possibility here that he doesn't follow up on—how elaborately might Jorge Luis Borges or Philip Roth, for example, have extended the situation of one writer finding himself in a place and a job that eerily paralleled that of his literary master.

Instead Fields expresses the parallels as awkward imitation, not reincarnation. He sees himself as a debased parody of Scott Fitzgerald rather than a replication, and Fields paints a picture of himself as a Fitzgerald manqué, minus the glamour, the literary credentials, the wit, the fame, or even the shell of dignity Fitzgerald wrapped around himself during his final stay in Hollywood. In short, Fields is to Fitzgerald what realism is to romanticism, a scruffy stand-in for an ideal.

In a larger sense, Yates is deflating a peculiarly Californian romantic ideal, turning the essentially homeless Fields into an examiner of the concept of home—California homes, American homes, and the idea of home in general. The first few paragraphs describe Fields's Manhattan home as a foul parody of the happy nuclear family's blessed domicile: "a dark, wretchedly cheap Greenwich Village apartment that had seemed good enough for holing up to get his work done after his marriage fell apart" (*LIL*, 213). His young daughters seem practically traumatized by the apartment's squalor when they visit him there—its dampness, its darkness, its hot and cold running cockroaches—and out of fatherly concern as much as careerism, he soon travels across the continent to replace the home, and the home life, he has lost. The word "home" pops up repeatedly during Jack's first date with Sally: "She would come home with him tonight," Yates says. "Sally said, 'We're practically home,' " "Woody came smiling home," "I feel at home here," "All the way home . . . he wanted to laugh," are only some of the repetitions in the four pages between their first drink together and their arrival at Fields's rented house (*LIL,* 218–22). The social critic James Howard Kunstler discusses the eagerness of Americans in particular to adorn sentimentally the idea of "home": "The prospective buyer was encouraged to think of his purchase as a *home,* with all the powerful associations the word dredges up from the psyche's nether regions; the seller was encouraged to think of it as a house, just a thing made of wood where the family happened to sleep and eat, nothing to be attached to" (Kunstler, 165). Finally it is the subject of their sourest argument: "Everything may be sick and degenerate or whatever you want to call it in that house," Sally justifies her dimwitted, crass housemates to Jack. "But it's my home."

That word ignites an explosion under Jack. "What do you mean, 'home,' for Christ's sake? That fucking menagerie couldn't be anybody's home" (*LIL,* 245). The word recurs again and again, until Jack finally returns back east. "Saying Goodbye to Sally" is Yates's longest story, and through its 70 pages we are aware that Jack will, as the title assures us, break up with Sally.

When he first gets to California, he stays for a while in the "sumptuous Malibu home" of the director of his screenplay, Carl Oppenheimer (*LIL,* 215). Here, Yates only flimsily disguises the use of his own life. The director of *Lie Down in Darkness* was to have been John Frankenheimer, whose biography was in every way identical to Carl Oppenheimer's: both Frankenheimer and Oppenheimer were, in the spring of 1962, 32-year-old *wunderkinder* fresh out of directing TV dramas of the 1950s. Like Yates's ostensibly fictional creation, Frankenheimer lived on the beach in Malibu, had two children, and with the exception of his being a Williams College graduate rather than a Yale man, the most significant distinction between the fictional creation and his counterpart seems to be the difference in the names Frankenheimer and Oppenheimer.

Fields's own name plays counterpoint to the concept of "home." A field is the polar opposite of a home, and the rootless Fields may be fated to live his life without any secure sense of what it means to have a home. Oppenheimer shares few of Fields's questions about his uprooted life.

Unlike Fields, Oppenheimer copes with his own divorce and estrangement from his children easily. He has a live-in girlfriend and doesn't quite understand why Fields needs to introduce complications into an otherwise uncomplicated life. When Oppenheimer invites Fields to bring Sally to a cocktail party, Fields tries to explain that "It's very—it's pretty complicated." Fields's love of overcomplication is clear in his need to find the precise distinction between "very complicated" and "pretty complicated"; the Oppenheimers of this world see no such valid distinction: "'Oh, Jesus, writers,' Oppenheimer said in exasperation, 'I don't know what the hell's the matter with you guys. Why can't you just get laid like everybody else?'" (*LIL,* 255).

A typical guilt-ridden Yates protagonist, Fields seeks explanations that place blame at his feet. He knows this tendency, articulates it, yet can't cure his obsessive introspection. When he and Sally start their love affair, Fields tries to guard against what he calls "worrying too soon"— worrying, that is, about disasters that are only mathematically possible (*LIL,* 227). After his first weekend with Sally, a completely satisfactory weekend idyll that makes him want "to laugh aloud because this was the way things should have been in his life: good money coming in, a weekend coming up, and a girl coming out to love him at the shore of the Pacific Ocean," Fields chooses to focus on the potential for disaster: "he began to be afraid they would never have such a good time again" (*LIL,* 222–23, 229).

No matter how pleasant his life is at the moment, Fields can always foresee some problem, and he can try to stave it off, and in that attempt he can always destroy his pleasure. Having eagerly and successfully pursued Sally Baldwin, he promptly locates some new sources of anxiety: "he'd decided it would be much better if Sally lived in a regular apartment, like a regular secretary" (*LIL,* 227). Sally actually lives much better than a regular secretary, in a large private apartment in a spacious mansion owned by a wealthy friend, but Fields concentrates on the lack of privacy, the vacuity of the household's other occupants, instead of enjoying his much-delayed gratifications. This habitual manufacturing of problems explains Yates's reputation as a profoundly gloomy writer. In the best of circumstances, disaster is never far away.

Immediately following Jack Fields's concerns about the unsuitability of Sally's apartment, he catches himself obsessing, but fixates only on the timing of his worries, not the worries themselves: "All his life, it now seemed, he had spoiled things for himself by worrying too soon" (*LIL,* 227). Worrying, in other words, is always appropriate. The only live question is when to worry, not whether to worry. Worrying as much as possible, Jack Fields can't conceive of someone like the carefree, successful Carl Oppenheimer. Jack wonders if this trait can be accurately summed up in a pop-psych catchphrase of the times: "Maybe—and this was a phrase then popular in national magazines—he was a self-destructive personality" (*LIL*, 217).

Yates's self-critical protagonists pick at their scabs and worry them, searching desperately for something they did that caused their suffering; and they won't stop until they locate that something, even though during the search they may have come across numerous likelier sources of the particular problem. Fields is pleased with himself when the affair with Sally gets off to a bright start, "as calm and strong and full of blood as if the notion of his being a self-destructive personality had never occurred to him. He was all right," he tells himself, using the catchphrase that, in *Liars in Love,* forebodes disaster (*LIL*, 218). Near the story's end, though, he is suddenly reconsidering whether "he might be a self-destructive personality after all," finally consoling himself with the thought that "any number of sanctimonious people had agreed to hang that bleak and terrible label on Scott Fitzgerald too" (*LIL*, 242).

Long as it is, "Saying Goodbye to Sally" is short on plot—seventy pages seems a lot of room for a writer to bed a secretary and then leave her—but Yates's protagonists react more than they act. Fields must respond to the actions of the subplot characters, the cohabitants of Sally's "home," whose boorish behavior prompts him to realize how little respect he has for her. These characters warrant little sympathy— they're cartoonish boobs—although one of them, a sullen preadolescent boy, does seem, by dint of his age, more a victim of the boorish culture around him than a cause of it. Like the plot in "Oh, Joseph, I'm So Tired," this subplot concerns a fatherless boy's bond with a man his self-centered mother soon rejects, little realizing the damage she's doing to her own child. Here as elsewhere Yates's portrayal of the inarticulate pain of a fatherless child is rendered with pathos.

Unfriendly Friends

"Trying Out for the Race" is told from the perspective of such a child, and it, like virtually every story in *Liars in Love,* describes the breakup of a relationship. But the relationship here is, nominally, not a romantic one. Russell Towers, a nine-year-old boy, is living with his divorced

mother and 13-year-old sister in 1935, when Russell's mother gets the
idea that she can live cheaper and better by sharing suburban quarters
with another single mother. The odd ménage, and the story, come to an
end after the other mother realizes that Lucy Towers wants much more
than a roommate.

Lucy Towers invents a close friendship between herself and the other
mother, Elizabeth Baker, a newswoman as focused and independent as
Lucy is fuzzy-headed and clinging. When Lucy phones with the proposal to merge households, Elizabeth, expecting a call from a man, is
disappointed to learn it "was Lucy Towers, one of her most admiring
friends, and this meant she would be on the damned phone for at least
an hour" (*LIL*, 68). Abstract nouns in each story—"home" in "Saying
Goodbye to Sally," "romance" in "Regards at Home," "art" in "Oh,
Joseph, I'm So Tired," "friendship" here—deceive Yates's weaker characters and expose their lies. For the self-deceiving Lucy, "friends" conjures
up all sorts of warm but false associations that the unromantic Elizabeth
can see right through. When Lucy tries to persuade her not to move
out, her final appeal is "besides, you and I are friends" (*LIL*, 85).

Throughout the story, Yates plants subtle gender confusions, such as
the description of Elizabeth pulling off her driving gloves "with an
unconscious little flourish, like that of a cavalry officer just dismounted
and removing his gauntlets after a long, hard ride" (*LIL*, 66). The word
"his," instead of some gender-neutral construction that the craftsman
Yates could easily have chosen, is in that sentence to drive eyebrows up.

The structure of the paragraphs in "Trying Out for the Race"
accounts for much of Yates's ironic tone. It was his pattern to build to a
climax and then, at the last moment, undercut the very point he'd built
up to. In Lucy's proposal of her housing scheme, for example, Yates
quotes at length her meandering chatter, as she rationalizes the merger
of the two broken families, blathering about phony issues of real estate
and location ("First of all, do you know those houses along the Post
Road in Scarsdale?"), and finally concluding with Lucy's emotional
needs that drive the whole bargain along: "'Oh, and besides,' Lucy con-
cluded, coming to the real point at last, 'besides, I'm awfully tired of living alone, Elizabeth. Aren't you?'" (*LIL*, 69).

That little repetition of Lucy's "besides," appearing at the end of one
speech segment and again at the beginning of the next, so subtle it
might seem to be a typo or an author's oversight if it is noticed at all,
underscores her desperate need to seem casual. By placing this line at
the end of a long, loopy speech and immediately before a space break in

the story, Yates lends it just the modicum of added weight to force the conclusion that Lucy's final phrase is far more than an afterthought. Lonely but without any true hope of attracting another husband, she wants to live with Elizabeth because Elizabeth is as close to a man as Lucy is likely to get. When Elizabeth announces the breakup of their household, Lucy feels betrayed because she has deluded herself that the ménage was a stable one. Blaming her failed marriage on some imagined inherent defect of men in general, Lucy believes she is protected from such disappointment by living with a woman, but as Elizabeth leaves her, "Lucy felt as if a man were leaving her" (*LIL,* 85).

Lucy is the least likely person in Yates's world to perceive the lesbian overtones in her admiration for Elizabeth. "If self-deception is an illness," Yates reminds us, "she was well into its advanced stages" (*LIL,* 68). And if a blind man on a galloping horse could spot Elizabeth's masculine traits, that by no means signifies that Lucy can. Here again, the subtle use of one of the most common English words tells Yates's reader details about Lucy that Lucy will never know. Notice the use of the word "and" in this description of Elizabeth's current lover: "He was often weak with ambition and anger and alcohol, and Elizabeth had come to love him for it" (*LIL,* 67). That final "and," used precisely where the word "but" belongs, characterizes both lovers. Elizabeth loves him because he's weak and malleable, and her need to be in control attracts him as well. Lucy is also weak and malleable, which is why Elizabeth agrees to move in with her.

Their children maintain a similar dynamic. The difference between the two generations of weak Towers in this tale is that Lucy's son, Russell Towers, acknowledges his weak character, suggesting that at nine years old he is more self-aware and more capable of self-criticism than his mother. His crisis comes when Nancy, Elizabeth's daughter, threatens to publicize in school that Russell is a sissy. He counteracts this lie by doing exactly what a sissy does with a problem: he tells his mother about it. To Russell's eventual horror, and the reader's immediate one, Lucy turns on Nancy and berates her harshly, humiliating the girl, who takes the rebuke in silence and in tears. Ostensibly spoken to win a measure of justice for her maligned son, Lucy's tirade leaves no doubt that it is intended to avenge, instead, her own humiliation at Nancy's mother's hands.

The children in this story need protection desperately, but the best source of certain types of protection—the children's fathers—is gone, and the substitute their mothers provide is, in this instance at least, wildly inappropriate. Because Elizabeth can fill the traditional paternal role comfortably, Nancy gets better protection than Russell, but the price of this protection is that Elizabeth also feels easy fulfilling a less admirable traditional male tendency, that of neglecting the emotional needs of the child. Both Elizabeth's emotional distance and Lucy's often smothering closeness are finally inadequate substitutes for having a male figure around.

Another brilliantly anticlimactic paragraph, describing Elizabeth's stance on marriage, motherhood, divorce, and parenting, concludes on a wonderfully sour note: "But now she was thirty-six, with nothing to do at the end of most days but go home to an upstairs apartment in New Rochelle and pretend to take pleasure in her child" (*LIL,* 66). At breakfast with Lucy and her children, Elizabeth complains of Nancy, "Sometimes I wish that child were at the bottom of the sea," challenging the silent table to defend Nancy's misbehavior or to criticize Elizabeth's concept of motherhood (*LIL,* 72).

Despite Lucy's weakness in dealing with Elizabeth and her weakness in bullying Nancy, she is all Russell has to rely on, so he relies on her but grows up mistrusting his own judgment in doing so. For this self-doubting child, the option of relying on his unreliable mother is only slightly less terrifying than relying on himself. Russell makes friends with Harry Snyder, a slightly older boy. One day, as they are playing with tin soldiers, something happens to inform Russell about his own character. When Harry's mother interrupts their play and tries to end it, Harry throws a full-fledged, out-of-control temper tantrum, similar in force and sheer childishness to a tantrum of Russell's, which was just detailed on the previous page. As with the bond of virginity between Privates Colby and Mueller, these acts of immaturity might have served to bond the two boys even closer but for a typical Yatesian turn: in Russell's tantrum he had been screaming at his mother, as she prepared to go out for the evening, "You *can't* go! You *can't* go!" The comparison ends with Russell's sickening realization: "Harry had cried because he wanted his mother to leave him alone; Russell had cried because he didn't—and therein lay the very definition of a mother's boy" (*LIL,* 75). Russell finds the small but vital distinction that will enable him to despise his own actions.

In the novel *A Special Providence* the protagonist's mother, interestingly enough, habitually worked herself up to the sort of temper tantrum that the son has here: "As if shot, she then clutched her left breast and collapsed full length on the floor. . . . She lay face down, quivering all over and making spastic little kicks with her foot" (*ASP*, 16). Here Russell is described similarly: "He faked a collapse on the floor, as if tantrums were a form of epileptic seizure" (*LIL*, 74). Embarrassing enough in an "often hysterical woman," this learned behavior is absolutely mortifying in a man of almost any age or temperament, barring him from the respect of any witness to it. Failing to attain dignity is implied in the title, which refers to Russell's failure to pass the try-out for the human race.

The relationship between a self-critical boy and his self-deceiving mother is explored at greater depth in "Regards at Home," where Yates's 23-year-old narrator has made career choices no better than his daft mother's.

Yates's protagonists take pride in never lying to themselves, but telling the truth to oneself often means acknowledging occasions in the past when one has lived a lie. That is to say, Yates's characters often stink with pride for having recognized their flaws, and the less admirable characters—mothers always and wives often—are monstrous not because they make mistakes but because they remain self-righteous about their reasons for having made them.

Yates worried that autobiographical fiction could serve therapeutic rather than fictional purposes.[10] "Trying Out for the Race," for example, could be read as a continuation of an argument with his mother, piling up evidence against her he was unable to articulate at Russell's age. Editors sometimes failed to understand why Yates's fiction took the shapes it did. When *The New Yorker* rejected this story, its fiction editor, Roger Angell, noted that the 1930s setting seems arbitrary. "Trying Out for the Race," Angell implied, was a simple story about adult cruelties still being practiced in 1979, so he questioned why Yates set this tale four decades earlier. If he wasn't just disingenuously reaching for a reason to reject the story, Angell certainly should have known that Yates worked on a principle contrary to *The New Yorker*'s. Angell, quite rightly considering the story's needs first, operated off a sound Occam-like principle of, whenever possible, selecting *New Yorker* stories set in the present, in the United States, and so forth.

Yates had his own Occam's razor, however, which stated that every invented (as opposed to remembered) detail that appears in a story detracts, bit by bit, from that story's authenticity and therefore is to be avoided wherever possible. Yates stuck stubbornly to the actual remembered details because purely invented ones would have encouraged him to state facile and unearned conclusions. Mistrusting artistry, Yates felt much more constrained than most fiction writers in sticking as closely as he could to the actual events that inspired him. The fiction writer's job, as he saw it, was to select and embroider details, not to weave fiction from whole cloth. As Angell implied, this philosophy occasionally results in plots that ramble around a story's themes rather than reinforcing them. "Trying Out for the Race" may be one of those occasions.

A Willing Suspension of Belief

Around the time Yates changed the title of the collection from *Broken Homes* to *Liars in Love,* he seems to have changed the title story's name from "New Friends" to "Liars in Love" as well, a far more ambiguous and potentially nastier title: it could simply mean that this is a story about two people who both tell lies and fall in love. The liars of the title are a married American writer whose wife has abandoned him in London and the young English prostitute he takes up with. (The prostitute, Christine, seems to believe she loves the protagonist, Warren Mathews, while Mathews instantly recognizes his loving responses as lies.) *Liars in Love* could also mean that to be in love is to be a kind of liar, and that love is in itself a kind of lie. The only difference between Christine's sincerity and Warren's lack of sincerity is that she is more capable of deceiving herself. Like another English girl, Jane Pringle in *Young Hearts Crying,* Christine embroiders her nonstop chatter with fanciful observations and downright fabrications on matters large and small. She invents stories—about the father of her child, or the histories of the other girls in the house she works out of, or her own past—and then takes Warren's half-bored attempt to clarify details as her cue to stage an indignant scene. He quickly looks for ways to break off with her but, at the same time, comes up with flimsy pretexts to avoid breaking up just yet.

The plot is resolved, not when the protagonist acts on his desire to break up, but when he passively finds himself overly involved in his lover's complicated living arrangements (as in "Saying Goodbye to Sally"). That false issue lets him sidestep the real problem and break up with her cleanly. The real problem—in "Liars in Love," the hopeless lack of commonality between an American intellectual and a British prostitute—is never addressed, which is another level of meaning in the title: the emotional stakes of love are so high that lovers often feel they must deceive themselves and others in order to tolerate the real risks.

So Warren Mathews vacillates while he finds just the right moment to say just the right words in exactly the right setting, but of course that perfect moment never comes. He is primarily concerned with giving a good performance as he breaks off with her—he catches himself rehearsing farewell speeches on the bus, replete with hand gestures. Many of his best chances seem to arise on the phone, where, he rationalizes, Christine won't be getting the full benefit of his performance, so he postpones it until he can do it as a live show.

As with "A Compassionate Leave," much of "Liars in Love" takes place while the action of the story is suspended. Warren's wife leaves London at the beginning of the story, but it is not clear to Warren or the reader whether she has left him permanently. The affair with Christine takes place as a substitute for resolving the more serious issues of the marriage. As soon as Warren does end the affair, after shilly-shallying for months on end, the real issue gets resolved, as if by magic: Warren's wife offers to give their marriage a second chance.

The plot is simple: Mrs. Mathews leaves Mr. Mathews and, after he diverts himself with a meaningless affair, she takes him back. The ridiculous nature of the affair, and the person he has it with, contrast with the larger issues at stake in the serious relationship—those of honesty and the long odds on achieving it.

Christine and Warren lie to each other routinely, as befits her profession, and Warren's pattern with his wife is also fundamentally built on lies. They travel to England at the start of the story, looking for relief from their crumbling marriage, which they can't bear to fight over or even to talk about. In the cramped English apartment they bump into each other—"'Oh, sorry,' they would mutter after each clumsy little bump or jostle. 'Sorry . . .'"—masking their hostility with polite words (*LIL*, 96). Like so many Yates characters, they feel far more comfortable playing roles than they do examining their realities.

In "Liars in Love," as in virtually all of Yates's work, the dominant metaphor is that of theater and movies and acting generally. When Warren's wife breaks the news to him that she is leaving him, the subject is couched in theatrical metaphors: she "tried to rehearse her lines just under her breath, but when the time came it proved to be a much less difficult scene than she had feared" (*LIL*, 97). Most significant of all is that Yates's characters have to talk themselves into feeling in love. "It may not have been love," Yates describes a very similar marriage at an earlier stage in "Regards at Home," "but we couldn't have been persuaded of that because we kept telling each other and telling ourselves it was" (*LIL*, 184).

The marriage in "Regards at Home" is, for all practical purposes, the same one in "Liars in Love." Only the names are changed; but the two marriages share a single dynamic, and "Regards at Home" ends where

"Liars in Love" begins: a young writer takes his wife and newborn daughter to Europe in the early 1950s, precisely as Yates did with his wife and newborn daughter.

"Regards at Home" and "Oh, Joseph, I'm So Tired," both published in the *Atlantic Monthly,* are the most clearly autobiographical stories in *Liars in Love,* if only because they share a narrator whom Yates acknowledged as his alter ego. Discussing autobiographical writing in an interview with *Contemporary Authors,* Yates confessed, "I had to wait a long time before I could see things in the round that occurred when I was seven years old." The Grove family of "Regards at Home" is identical to the Grove family in *A Good School,* and Yates goes on to say, "The family in *A Good School* is the same family in 'Oh, Joseph, I'm So Tired.' The father and brother and sister and mother are all the same people" (Ross, 535).

This narrator identifies himself only as "Billy" in "Oh, Joseph, I'm So Tired," which is set in early 1933 when he is only seven years old, but in *A Good School* and "Regards at Home" he gives his name as William Grove. Yates explored possible alter egos before settling on Grove, who, Brooks Landon noted, "seems to overlap an earlier Yates character, Robert Prentice, protagonist of *A Special Providence* (1969) and of the story 'Builders' in *Eleven Kinds of Loneliness* (1962). Yates has called 'Builders' 'A direct autobiographical blowout.'"[11]

Close to Home

"Regards at Home" is about art and artlessness. One of Yates's most direct questionings of his feelings about art, it begins with 23-year-old Bill Grove meeting his cubicle-mate in the public relations section of a New York City corporation, where Grove has just been hired to produce the copy for "a slick and unreadable house organ" (*LIL,* 177). Producing the artwork is the job of his co-worker Dan Rosenthal, who has been drawing and designing for the firm for an unspecified time when the story begins in the spring of 1949. A "year or so older" than Grove, Dan Rosenthal takes the initiative in introducing himself to Grove, whose shyness is common to virtually all of Yates's protagonists (*LIL,* 177).

From the beginning, the outsider Grove admires the more graceful Rosenthal—again, Yates's other protagonists, particularly his youthful ones, attach themselves to some idealized, slightly older form of themselves. What Grove admires most about Rosenthal is his ability "to talk and listen while executing even the subtlest part of his work" (*LIL,* 177).

Although he lacks respect for the writing he's doing, Grove is dismayed at the effort he must devote to it. He's the grown-up version of the awkward protagonist of *A Good School,* a craftsman who has yet to master survival skills. Rosenthal's effortless competence, like that of the cleverer Dorset boys, stands out from Grove's painstaking effort. Grove must actually extend himself to do hackwork, and he studies Rosenthal to learn how to do corporate work with less effort. There is never any question that their jobs should, or even could, be done well—their stated goal, after all, is to produce a journal that is "unreadable." Of all the friends–*cum*–role models in Yates—Harry Snyder, George Mueller, and John Cabot in this volume alone—Dan Rosenthal is the most wholesome, and "Regards at Home" is the most optimistic story in the book.

Grove envies Rosenthal's mastery of craft and, moreover, his modesty about it. Up to this point, Grove's only model of artistic comportment has been his mother, a "bewildered, rapidly aging, often hysterical woman who had always considered herself a sculptor with at least as much intensity as I brought to the notion of myself as a writer" (*LIL,* 179).

This is a frightening realization. Grove's mother, like the sculptor mothers in *A Special Providence,* "Oh, Joseph, I'm So Tired" and elsewhere, is a failed artist and a failed person, and Grove seems to have hitched his wagon to her rapidly descending star. The optimism in "Regards at Home" results from the psychomachia: The good angel Rosenthal wins out here over the sinister Mrs. Grove.

His mother romantically idealizes her own problems, turning them into virtues. Poverty, for example, is good because it leads to adventure, and wearing ragged clothes and going hungry for days on end is a small part of what Grove, paraphrasing his mother, calls the "romance of our lives" (*LIL,* 180). Others have told Grove of her flaws—his divorced and now-dead father had appraised her values as "childish and irresponsible" and Grove's girlfriend flatly terms her "an art bum"—but Rosenthal is the only one who shows him a way out of her clutches (*LIL,* 180, 184). He encourages Grove to hone his craft. By the story's end he does, and he marries his girlfriend and escapes to Europe. "I wanted to put three thousand miles of sea between my mother and myself," he acknowledges midway through the story, when he is trying to con Rosenthal into praising his fictitious drawing ability so he might study art in Paris (*LIL,* 197). In the end Grove makes it to Europe, but he does it on his own merits, and he leaves feeling pleased with himself, a rarity in a Yates story ending.

The Cost of Lies

Another story about Grove and his mother, "Oh, Joseph, I'm So Tired," ends bleakly. In early 1933 the narrator's mother, a struggling and none-too-talented artist, uses some connections to sculpt a bust of the newly elected President Roosevelt. To allow her the time to sculpt, she hires a tutor for her children, but when she returns from Washington, disappointed by the casual reception her artwork has received from the president, she learns that the tutor has been bragging about having been saved from the Great Depression by some "rich, dumb, crazy woman who's paying him to tutor her kids" (*LIL,* 29). Although the narrator plainly adores this tutor, she fires him immediately, dropping some choice anti-Semitic remarks in the process.

Yates's reliance on his own personal history is clear here: his mother was a sculptor who did present FDR with a bust in early 1933, when Yates, like Billy Grove in "Oh, Joseph, I'm So Tired," was seven years old; the less easily documented characters and events are much likelier to have been recreated from Yates's memory than invented from whole cloth.

The plot twist here is typically contrived, resting on the sheer coincidence that the friend who recommends her for the president's commission is the same friend who recommends her children's tutor, thus making possible the chain of gossip that reaches her ears inadvertently. Moreover, the language that so offends her—the phrase "a rich, dumb, crazy woman"—is clearly the gossiper's paraphrase, remembered weeks after the actual conversation, and not the exact wording of the tutor, who seems elsewhere to be a polite young man and genuinely grateful for the job. He might very well have phrased that same thought in far less offensive words, as any reasonable person would conclude on hearing that snippet of gossip. But Mrs. Helen Grove is no reasonable person.

Her son's characterization of her, in fact, is of a deranged woman. The crucial turn in "Oh, Joseph, I'm So Tired" is not the turn of plot itself, but the paranoid imposition of a plot—in both the fictional sense and the psychological one—by the narrator's mother. If her own life's work has come to nothing—and after her final presentation of the bust, it seems that it has—someone must take the blame, and she lacks the courage to do it. Instead, she makes a scapegoat of the children's tutor. "Oh, Joseph, I'm So Tired" is a panel in Yates's lifelong portrait of his mother's character and lack thereof, a campaign carried out so relentlessly over such a period of time as to amount to character assassination.

"Oh, Joseph, I'm So Tired" focuses on the mother's lashing out against one of her seven-year-old son's potential father substitutes, who abound in this short story: the boy's father himself, who is an active presence and a minor character in the story's plot; the tutor, a young Dutch Jew named Bart Kampen; an older neighbor boy, named John Cabot; the mother's lover, an Englishman named Eric Nicholson; and President Roosevelt. Because of the strict protocol of behavior with the president, which Mrs. Grove all too eagerly violates, her interaction with Roosevelt gives the most obvious example of her inappropriate behavior.

The first words out of her mouth to the president are "I didn't vote for you, Mr. President. I'm a good Republican and I voted for President Hoover" (*LIL,* 11). Presuming Roosevelt cares about her voting record, she expands on it. A similar exchange takes place in Gore Vidal's *The Best Man,* where a private citizen, played by Shelly Berman in the film version, at the end of a once-in-a-lifetime meeting with a president, informs him, "I didn't vote for you the second time, sir, you see." As an aide gives him the bum's rush, the president gravely counsels him, "Let your vote remain between you and your God." The presumption of both the Berman character and Mrs. Grove is that the president would care a whit how they voted.

By firing Bart Kampen, Mrs. Grove tries to assert her position in the social pecking order. If the world at large ignores her, humiliates her, and makes her eat her peck of dirt, then she is going to locate some poor sad nobody over whom she has power and do the same to him, even if it means doing the greatest harm to her own son, who admires Kampen and who desperately needs a father figure to make their Greenwich Village apartment into a home.

The narrator's mother is the world's worst judge of character, as witnessed by her love affair with Eric Nicholson. An Englishman who tries to provide culture around the household in the form of cartoons from *Punch,* partial editions of Dickens, fishing gear, and the like, Nicholson shows little affection for the children upon whom he bestows these gifts. The gifts impress the foolish Mrs. Grove, as Nicholson intends, while Billy and his older sister remain puzzled by the largely unusable trinkets. Finally, tired of impressing Helen Grove, Eric Nicholson suddenly abandons the Grove family to return to England and the wife who, it turns out, he had never actually divorced. This type of cad recurs in several other works—most notably, as Sterling Nelson in *A Special Providence*—suggesting that Yates had drawn from life this portrait of a facile

Brit exploiting an American woman's pretentious yearnings. The men-
dacious suavity of this type easily cons the narrator's mother, who pays
keen attention to superficial manners, and to "breeding" and "aristoc-
racy," but has no judgment for real character.

Seven-year-old Billy Grove recoils from this English windbag standing in for his absent father, and he is finally denied Bart Kampen's
fatherly qualities. Billy nurtures a friendship with an older boy, John
Cabot, also fatherless but more assured than Billy—another in a series
of slightly older, more self-assured role models that runs through many
of Yates's works. Such characters find themselves providing the Yates
character with an ideal to follow and, in most cases, ultimately to be disappointed by. John Cabot's traits seem ideal for him to serve as Billy's
friend: he is athletic, well-dressed, popular, all the things the shy, stut-
tering Billy Grove is not. Yet he uses his athleticism to kill Billy's pet
fish, and his assuredness lets him look up Billy's sister's skirt.

Because of the father's sporadic appearance in the boy's life, he is a
kind of father substitute as well. He is hardly around, and Billy misses
him more than he knows: when he is there Billy plainly worships him.
There is no ambivalence about Billy's father in "Oh, Joseph, I'm So
Tired," as there is in other works, in which Yates often assigns some of
the damage caused by his parents' divorce to his father, either for being
absent or for having contributed to the breakup (as in *A Good School* or
the early uncollected story "Lament for a Tenor"), but here his seven-
year-old narrator bears all the weight. In one touching scene, the father
has stored some stamps for the children in a pocket, but he leaves without remembering to give them their gift. When Billy and his sister
remember, calling, "Daddy! Daddy! You forgot the stamps," they find
his cheeks soaked with tears (*LIL,* 8). Embarrassed, the children grab
the stamps and run off without acknowledging his loneliness. Elsewhere
the children see his humane side as they hear him praise FDR, look with
compassion on the homeless, and set himself apart from his ex-wife's
ridiculous aristocratic pretensions.

"Oh, Joseph, I'm So Tired" has a large and complicated cast of characters—it is probably Yates's most fully textured short story—and one
of the most sharply drawn characters is the mother's close friend "Sloane
Cabot": "She'd once confided to my mother that she'd made up both her
names: 'Sloane' because it sounded masculine, the kind of name a
woman might need for making her way in the world, and 'Cabot'
because—well, because it had a touch of class. Was there anything
wrong with that?" (*LIL,* 10). That last rhetorical question sounds as

smarmy as the "Saturday Night Live" parody of Harvey Fierstein—"I just wanna be loved. Is that so wrrrrrong?" What's so wrong about Mrs. Grove's appropriating her oppressors's Episcopalianism and Republicanism and Anglophilia, and what's so wrong about her friend appropriating a Boston Brahmin name, is that it's a lie. It stems from no deeply held beliefs, political or religious or otherwise, but from a dizzy and dangerous idea of one's own classiness. Sloane Cabot—we never do learn what her real name is—wants the advantages of belonging to the upper classes but doesn't see the need to have earned them, and she certainly doesn't counsel everybody to take her course. She, like Billy's mother, considers herself special, privileged, and entitled, and so the two women becomes fast friends.

Other than shared pretensions, their most valued connection is that both women place themselves far above their families and both women justify leading a life of lies by claiming the honorific *artists*. Sloane Cabot works as a secretary on Wall Street but shows contempt for the job: like other wanna-be artists and intellectuals in Yates, she writes radio scripts in the office when her boss is out of town. Her writing is god-awful, and condescending as well, as Billy learns when she has a script read aloud by their circle of friends, who are also the characters. Sloane's ineptness at stagecraft is obvious even to the little boy, who remembers being puzzled by the notion that anyone would want to listen to a series of meandering and unconnected vignettes, but he is more than just puzzled. Sloane Cabot has incorporated Billy's pronounced stutter into her radio script, and written it for the maximum comic effect. Worse, she doesn't seem to understand how a public reading of the script might hurt Billy's feelings. This trait sets the stage for Helen Grove's self-centered insensitivity in later firing the tutor her young children adore.

The language prefacing the radio script's dialogue typifies Sloane's dopey sense of being special: she describes the courtyard connecting their lower-middle-class Greenwich Village row houses as "enchanted" several times, and further glamorizes the residents as "an enchanted circle of friends" (*LIL*, 26). With this faulty premise, she aggrandizes her neighbors and depression life in general. In short, the radio script romanticizes life out of all proportion—that is all the script does, really—and though Billy's mother declares it "perfect," it of course gets instantly rejected, thus confirming to Sloane Cabot the insensitivity of commercial radio. A nice effect is achieved by subtle juxtaposition here. Right after Billy explains his deep feelings of shame at Sloane's characterization of him as a walking stutter, Billy's mother praises the effort:

"Oh, Sloane, that's marvelous. That's really exciting," not noticing or not caring about her son's wounded feelings (*LIL,* 28).

The real cost of these mothers' lying to each other about their artistic talent and their prospects for fulfilling it is not to themselves. Like the homeless men they resemble, Sloane Cabot and Helen Grove huddle around the flickering flame of their talents, trying to keep it alive by fanning it with their self-love, all the while keeping their own children outside their circle, leaving them to grow up with the knowledge that their mothers tried to nurture their careers instead of their children.

The mother's romanticism is as false as her weakly held religious sentiments. Yates detested religion equally with self-important fine art, and his titles often show his intense feelings. The title comes from a story Sloane Cabot tells at Christmas, about the Virgin Mary's suffering as she wandered homeless looking for some warm place to deliver the Christ child. Sloane clearly sees herself and her friend as suffering in poverty but knowing, as surely as Mary knows from having been assured by an angel, that all her suffering will be to her greater glory and, most satisfying of all, to humanity's redemption. All the pain her travails cause the child, Mary and Sloane and Helen persuade themselves, will make their ultimate redemption that much more striking.

It's all a lie, Yates concludes, a lie that lets such people ruin their lives and their families' lives, only so they might believe that they are somehow special and separate from the mass of suffering people. The titles *A Special Providence* and *The Easter Parade* share in this religious imagery, an imagery not of redemption but of self-told lies that encourage hypocrisy and selfish behavior.

Chapter 6

Chronicling and Confessing:
A Special Providence, The Easter Parade, Young Hearts Crying, Cold Spring Harbor

Despite consistent success with short novels and short stories, Yates felt compelled throughout his career to attempt longer, more ambitious novels. Sometimes these works were longer in their span of years, but they were always textured differently, taking a more comprehensive view of his personal history and the modern America that paralleled it.

Yates had a textbook case of second-novel blues after finishing *Revolutionary Road*. In 1960, on a fellowship application, he described plans for a second novel, this one about World War II: "the novel will consist of four parts. . . . owing to its autobiographical nature, I was reluctant to start work on it until I had first learned to write a more objective novel. That book *{Revolutionary Road}* is now finished" (BU-MM). Off and on through the 1960s Yates labored on this project, which publishers were hounding him for as early as 1963, and which emerged in 1969 as *A Special Providence*.

Revolutionary Road and *Eleven Kinds of Loneliness* proved to Yates that he could write fiction professionally. As the language of the fellowship application suggests, neither work drew on Yates's life story with particular faithfulness. Now, convinced of his professional detachment, Yates felt he could indulge in more overtly confessional material. *A Special Providence* is a rambling novel of development that follows the early life, adolescence, and World War II experiences of Bob Prentice, a thinly disguised Richard Yates. The book cuts across the depression years and into the mid-1940s, studying Bobby's frustrating relationship with his bohemian sculptress mother, Alice.

Several years later *The Easter Parade* (1976) would cut a wider swathe as it followed the Grimes sisters from their 1930s childhoods to the disillusionments of the 1960s. Yates focuses on Emily Grimes, the more complex of the two women, but he uses her roles as friend, student, lover, and daughter to study midcentury America. The confessional element in *The Easter Parade* is obscured by Yates's gender swap: Emily shares with Yates the experience of having been the younger of two siblings growing up in a broken home during the Great Depression, who later witnesses an older sister's decline. *The Easter Parade* is his speculation into the differences in his life had he been born a girl.

The time frame of *Young Hearts Crying* (1984) overlaps *The Easter Parade*. The plot begins just after World War II, when *The Easter Parade*'s chronicle is half over, and it stretches into the late 1970s, as the ardor and energy of Michael and Lucy Davenport ignites, fizzles, fades, and briefly flickers again. They start out as lovers at Harvard; thereafter they exemplify their times as they struggle to meet the demands of art and literature, love and friendship.

In his final completed book Yates again employed the long haul of the chronicle novel: *Cold Spring Harbor* (1986) is the story of two families, the Drakes and the Shepards, during the Great Depression and World War II. Yet another story of falling expectations, this account of Long Islanders and Manhattanites is an attempt, within some 200 pages, to represent two kinds of family failure: a Greenwich Village bohemian kind, seen in the behavior of Gloria Drake and her sensitive son, Phil; and a more ordinary suburban kind seen in the life of Captain Shepard and his roughneck boy, Evan. Gloria is Yates's final attempt to portray his mother and the destructive effect her narcissism bore on the world around her; this time, he varies the portrait by eliminating her artistic career, leaving her pervasive personality disorder unadorned.

Each of the books is a wide-angle picture of the American middleclasses; even a short volume like *Cold Spring Harbor* is tightly packed with observations about status distinctions, financial worries, jobs, and aspirations. Yet each is informed by the central obsessions of Richard Yates's own life: his parents' divorce, his mother's flightiness and sentimentality, his own fear of failure. The books have competing impulses within them: the private desire to process anxieties and the public ambition to survey the varieties of American weakness. These drives are skillfully combined in *The Easter Parade* and *Young Hearts Crying*, but in *A Special Providence* and *Cold Spring Harbor* they often work against each other, causing those books to seem curiously disunified. In *Young Hearts Crying* the poet Michael Davenport boasts of constructing poems that won't come apart; two of Yates's major novels do.

The Family Romance

The structure of *A Special Providence* highlights this weakness: sections devoted to Bob Prentice's home life alternate with sections about his World War II army service. The prologue, set in 1944, shows Prentice on a pass visiting his mother in New York. The chapter describes the mother's financial irresponsibility and artistic aspirations, the father's early death, the boy's complex responses to his ever-present mother. Alice—resented by her son as a sentimental egotist and at the same time romanticized by him as a free spirit—is the linchpin of the book. Having filled her boy with the idea that their life together is special, she shows where Yates gets his overarching theme: the irony of expectations. Sections of the book study the disappointments that the American class system has in store for this odd couple, and that the U.S. Army has in store for Bob Prentice on his own. At the prologue's end Bob sits at the window of his mother's Upper West Side apartment, taking stock of his disappointments: a grim dinner at Childs, the long bus ride to New York, the lifetime's worth of rage and love directed at an absurd parent.

Part 1 abruptly switches to a Virginia army camp. From this "Infantry Re-tread Center" to small German towns, the army material is unified, insofar as it is unified at all, by Bob's anxieties about himself.[1] Is he special—indeed, is he even adequate—to the tasks before him? This "wet-behind-the-ears young twerp of an incompetent" is Yates's embarrassingly personal version of himself; the central conflict is about how Bob is condescended to and humiliated by older army men (*ASP,* 30). His story is organized into a series of gaffes and mishaps. Bob becomes a runner for his platoon, only to be anxiously unclear as to where he is to run when the platoon is under attack. He becomes friends with the platoon intellectual, Quint, only to be told that he goofs off and talks too much. Like many Yates characters, Bob Prentice yearns for dignity and integrity—but gets mockery. He whimpers and whines and, at the end of the section, has collapsed altogether with pneumonia.

In part 2 Yates tells the misadventures of Alice and her son, generally using Alice as the center of consciousness. The book's strongest writing is to be found in the Greenwich Village, suburban, and Texas scenes. Yates follows Alice's trail of professional failures, unpaid bills, and romantic smash-ups. With a keen eye for a deflating detail and a fine sense of what constitutes domestic disaster, Yates lets Alice endure just about any slight available to a woman artist of small talent. A vulgar local doctor (complete with cheap cigars) with whom she has an affair fails to begin to understand her art; the kids in Connecticut mock her use of Bobby as a nude model; her patrons on the exclusive estate of Boxwood at Riverside sue her for back rent; her sympathetic friends, one of them a Marxist, offer only the weakest pity when disaster strikes.

Of all the let-downs Alice gets from friends, the most hurtful comes from her fancy English lover who, like the virtually identical English lover in "Oh, Joseph, I'm So Tired," sets her up in a nice Scarsdale house and then skips out, returning to the English wife he had claimed to have divorced. Left virtually penniless, Alice and Bobby wind up outside Austin, Texas, where they find out that Alice's sister and brother-in-law have little more sympathy or money to offer than her friends had. From their patrician landlady, the grand dame Mrs. Vander Meer, to the other extreme, Alice's boorish Texan in-law, mother and son run the gauntlet of American social humiliations. Yates's ironic catchphrase, repeated like a nightmarish mantra throughout his work, is on the tip of Alice's tongue: *Things will be all right,* she soothes Bobby one night as they settle down in a hotel after escaping the oppressive home of their relatives in Texas.

After this strong section, the writing in part 3 seems plodding. Bob's platoon drives across Europe, and his obsessions are along for the ride. In his best work, Yates generally avoids pat psychoanalytic generalizations (in *Disturbing the Peace,* he zings psychobabble cleverly and furiously), but here Bob's insecurities seem reductively parallel to his mother's in the previous section. Recovered from the setback that pneumonia dealt him, Bob finds that his platoon mates have forgotten him or, worse, confused him with an earlier and even more incompetent platoon screwup. Before he can hope to assert himself as a competent soldier or as a grown man, he finds he must assert his very identity, and he is frustrated and paralyzed with fear over asserting any of these things. Yates makes Bob Prentice into a sad case, as predictable in his tropism to failure as Walter Henderson. Afraid of "fucking up," Bob is belligerent about criticism, defensive about reprimands. When an officer upbraids him, partly misstating the case against Prentice but getting other parts right, Prentice argues with him. Although a simple "Yes, sir" would end the painful discussion, every word of Bob's arguing lowers him in the officer's regard.

At the same time, like Frank Wheeler in *Revolutionary Road,* he would like to admire himself. In a crucial scene, he takes his own measure in a mirror and enjoys the image of the powerful combat man he can make himself appear to be. But the narcissism altogether lacks charm or interest. (The cliché of the mirror scene, too, marks a rare lapse in Yates's professional judgment.) It's not the magnetic Frank Wheeler strutting his stuff, but a born loser briefly deceiving himself with his illusory appearance.

Besides this falling off, there is the raw unmediated quality of the story: rather than creating a clever image of his own insecurity, Yates provides a great deal of explicit (and fairly dull) material about his own vulnerability. The army scenes seem like stylized backdrops for an endless series of frustrations: the tests of one's manhood and integrity, the puerile macho rejection of feeling, the predictable scene (complete with what Jerome Klinkowitz aptly terms "cinema heroics") in which Bob Prentice rejects his own achievement (Klinkowitz, 33). Bob realizes how sentimental he had become about himself and his dignity when he gets into a fistfight and immediately afterward vomits. (The whole thing seems tough and self-critical but is ultimately sentimental, like similar scenes in *From Here to Eternity,* which it resembles). He's settled a difference fair and square with a regular-guy fight at the back of a barn. The trouble here is that garrulous Bob, unlike more mysterious Yates characters, disgorges everything, thus ruining the tension of the story.

The epilogue, dated 1946, returns to Alice's grim New York world and back to Yates's sharper, more resonant observations. We even return to Childs, where Alice and her sometime friend Natalie have come together to be lonely. Characteristically, Alice is happy that her Manhattan cocktail is two-thirds full. For her, everything in life has been two-thirds full. Unlike Bobby, she is a buoyant survivor whose self-deceptions are easier to take than his whining. This unintentional effect, of course, must have galled Yates, for in attempting to expose Alice, he actually memorialized her. Like the opening, the final pages contain strong material: Alice's weakness stays in the reader's mind. Her last wartime appearance had been on the Saturday night of Bob's weekend pass, but now, in 1946, it's Sunday—which is to say, a day to dress up for the Episcopal service at St. Thomas's, think about the past, and drink before going out to dinner. Yates's characteristic deflations are used to good effect. Alice's desperately upbeat thoughts are matched by perfectly timed disappointments, both large and small. Child's is "kind of nice," although "she used to think it was dreadful": there was a lot of "good nourishment" in chicken croquettes, if you swallowed carefully (*ASP,* 335–38).

This Yatesian technique, asserting something positive and then backing off, is everywhere. George Prentice has proposed that he and Alice get back together; his next appearance is in his coffin. The two-thirds-full Manhattan seems like a comfort until we hear about the alcoholic's bottle at home; and Bobby will return soon, except that Yates has him mailing her small sums from England while giving no sign of coming home. The quiet pain and denial of this ending make the furious combat sequences seem abstract and routine. Such confessional passages, despite their crude reductive quality, are much more memorable than full-dress accounts of army life. The two phases of Bob Prentice's story are also held together by no more than the vague theme of vulnerability. The intended novel of a young man's development—Yates's *Portrait of the Artist As a Young Man*—often switches unintentionally to the more riveting story of a middle-aged woman's struggle. And in the end Bob's purpose seems to be to reject his mother with brutal finality. Unlike other stark Yates endings, especially those in *Eleven Kinds of Loneliness,* this is flat and emotionless. It spoils a good final section.

Altogether *A Special Providence* fails as a novel while establishing Yates as a first-rate portraitist of a floundering woman. The book's sharpest passages show Alice divided between sentimentality and real poignancy, someone who loves Kate Smith's "When the Moon Comes Over the Mountain" and Keats's line about Ruth amidst the alien corn. Unlike shadowy theatrical April Wheeler or the sketches of women in *Eleven Kinds of Loneliness,* Alice is no mere creature of declamations and desperate measures. Yates also pulls back from making her a total washout as a sculptress. With her exhibit at the Whitney and her piece photographed for the *New York Times,* she is presented as a striver on the outskirts of Arttown. Such strivers, necessary to art but necessarily pathetic, always appealed to Yates as subject matter. In studying Alice Prentice and her kind, he has ample opportunity to chart the terms of embarrassment and qualified failure.

The Easter Parade: American Women at Midcentury

With *The Easter Parade* Yates uses a sharper focus and a larger canvas for chronicling and confessing. The female psyche is split into career woman Emily Grimes, hapless Long Island housewife Sarah Grimes, and their pretentious mother, Pookie. The time frame is an epic slice of American history in which the Grimes sisters, their parents, and their men, including Sarah's sons, are paraded before the reader in all their vanity and pathos. The book is new ground for Yates, his first attempt to view Americans across the years of war, depression, and prosperity. Although a mere 229 pages, it has a Tolstoyan sweep and an opening worthy of the Russian master: "Neither of the Grimes sisters would have a happy life, and looking back it always seemed that the trouble began with their parents' divorce" (*EP,* 3).

Yates's simplicity of statement, his ability to plunge from a stark generalization into a scene, and his telescoping of many lives make the book an ambitious, indeed grand, attempt to capture people against the backdrops of American history. Like Tolstoy packing in the copious social detail in "The Death of Ivan Illych," Yates presents the grim tale of the sisters' lives by locating them amid the bourgeois, often trivial conflicts of four decades. Mixing pop culture, intellectuals' literary and cultural currency, business talk, and the notation of the suburbs, Manhattan, and the midwest, Yates produces his most comprehensive account of American unhappiness. The book has the substantiality of *Revolutionary Road,* including the thick descriptions of ordinary days and the cool comprehension of two generations.

The three parts of the novel are tightly packed units. Part 1 extends from the 1930s and the sisters' childhood in Tenafly, New Jersey, and Larchmont, New York, to their young womanhood in Greenwich Village during the war. Yates accords each girl a defining romantic moment: the rather conventional Sarah gets involved with Tony Wilson, a smarmy, brutal Brit who dresses up on Easter Sunday 1941 in a cutaway and drives uptown with Sarah on public display in his convertible, causing the two of them to find themselves, as the song says, in the rotogravure. Emily, a serious girl, soon to be a scholarship student at Barnard, has her own equivalent of the Easter Parade—a bizarre encounter with a sailor who also takes her uptown (on a bus) and seduces her in Central Park. Later in part 1 both girls settle into marriage, Sarah with Tony, Emily with a neurotic philosophy instructor at Columbia. Yates neatly counterpoints the girls' experiences: sociopath Tony hates "coons, kikes, and Catholics" and beats his wife; Emily's sensitive intellectual Andrew Crawford is all tolerance and gentility but is disgusted by his wife's body.

Part 2 opens in the 1950s when Emily, by now the book's central character, has graduated from Barnard and taken a job with *Food Field Observer* (successor to Frank Wheeler's Knox Company in Yates's continuing series of hackwork jobs, just like the ones he held while writing *Revolutionary Road*). She also goes through two abortions, a serious affair with the poet Jack Flanders, and extended sojourns with him in Iowa and Europe.

This portion of the book is dotted with fragments: aborted literary ventures and broken attempts at love and home life. In 1955 Emily tries to write a magazine article on abortion. Later we hear about another piece she's planning about a New Yorker in the midwest. These fragments are also complemented by the lame attempts of the unsophisticated Sarah to set down on paper a history of one of her husband's ancestors; meanwhile, her marriage to Tony has turned into a nightmare of beatings that both partners hurry to conceal. Pookie moves into Great Hedges, Sarah's and Tony's Long Island house that she has pretentiously given its estatelike name. (Yates's mother, Ruth Maurer Yates, nicknamed "Dookie," had dubbed her daughter's married home "High Hedges.")[2] After suffering a stroke, Pookie winds up in a nursing home fantasizing about being President Kennedy's mother-in-law. By the end of this section, Emily is involved with a public relations man, Pookie has been transferred to the state institution at Central Islip, and Sarah is pathetically resisting the prospect of a separation from Tony.

Part 3 quickly passes over the early 1960s and begins with Emily's job opportunity in 1965. Her ad agency has the account for a new synthetic, and Emily gets to talk about legal issues with Howard Dunninger, a legal counsel to National Carbon. The question of misrepresentation of the new fabric and the synthetic idea feed nicely into two larger lies: Dunninger, a masterful professional whose suave manner and position suggest an end to Emily's string of wimpy boyfriends, is actually a prisoner of his ex-wife, and his affair with Emily turns out to be just another of her self-deceiving miscalculations. Something similarly false and creepy has always lurked beneath the civilized surface of Sarah's marriage, climaxing when the wretched Sarah, who has become little more than Tony's punching bag and then an alcoholic patient at Central Islip, dies at home after a puzzling fall down the stairs. Tony, under suspicion for murder, is cleared by the police but not by Emily.

The incompetent policework is the final malfeasance committed by men in *The Easter Parade*. Yates holds back on forming any formulaic conclusion, but it's inescapable how culpable the men in *The Easter Parade* are, in various forms: they are impotent intellectuals (Andrew Crawford) or resentful artists (Jack Flanders) or useless sex machines (Emily's ultimately homosexual lover Lars Ericson) or yahoos (Tony) or blobs of proletarian protoplasm (Sarah's sons, Tony Jr. and Eric) or manipulative weaklings (Howard Dunninger). The final section leaves us with Emily bringing up the rear of this gruesome Easter Parade of disappointment and betrayal. Beaten down by life, her career in shards, Emily arrives at her nephew Peter Wilson's house in New Hampshire practically begging for alms, and the kindly young man takes in his bewildered aunt.

Though Yates's work has been characterized as hostile to women (his relentless depictions of his mother being the chief evidence of such characterization), here he has composed a work that, had it been published by a woman, might have been acclaimed as a feminist classic of the 1970s.[3] Emily Grimes is easily his most rounded portrait of any female character; her bitterness and her confusion over what, exactly, went wrong in her life are convincing without the least condescension.

The Easter Parade's theme of incompleteness contrasts with the seeming completeness of the literally picture-perfect appearance of Tony and Sarah in Easter 1941. The novel's title has purely upbeat connotations, yet throughout the book promising event after promising event fizzles into disappointment, and the title finally forms a Yatesian paradigm of deflation. Other Yates titles take similar forms: in *Eleven Kinds of Loneliness,* for example, the positive-sounding titles "The Best of Everything," "Out with the Old," "Fun with a Stranger," and "A Really Good Jazz Piano" precede stories of unremitting bleakness.

Yates's ironic allusions to religious faith also recur in other titles: the "special providence" that Bob Prentice's mother proclaims for her son is empty chatter and mere wishful thinking. In *The Easter Parade* Emily survives one little death after another and is resurrected into a new life again and again. But the down tone of the ending suggests that her promisingly helpful Christian nephew will prove as hypocritically unkind as the other men in the book have been. Though Yates occasionally alludes to religious uplift and hope of redemption, he views that prospect with skepticism. As it was to young Bobby Prentice, its promise had been held out before Yates many a time, but it never came to him unpolluted by human folly. Easter does not represent eternal hope in this book as much as it represents that guarded hope mixed with the sordid reality of cheap newspaper photos, popular show tunes, and the superficial bright smiles of a couple embarking on a ruinous marriage.

There are other unsatisfying attempts at harmony here: Andrew Crawford completes his psychoanalysis, which, far from making him a better person, causes him to punish Emily with his self-indulgent honesty; Jack Flanders finishes the book he's struggling with, but for all his effort, it is harshly treated by the critics; Howard Dunninger resurrects his (as Emily thought) dead-and-buried first marriage. Throughout *The Easter Parade* Yates shows unfinished business and fragmentary encounters, from Emily's comic yet terrifying awakening beside a sleeping stranger to her ridiculously incomplete articles to Sarah's botched marriage.

Yates seems to be working with an irony out of Tolstoy: triviality meeting profundity. The title character of Tolstoy's "The Death of Ivan Illych" never brings anything important to fruition; his relationships with his wife and son are short-circuited; his legal clients are always unable to get across their meaning and the human dimension of their cases. The only things that are finished are the mundane and the deeply spiritual: Ivan's house decorations and the realization of his mortality. Yates's imagination runs along the same lines; the perfect scene in the rotogravure, as well as the scene of the ideal couple in interlocked arms as they toast each other—these are the trivial accomplishments that Yates leaves us to compare with the general mess of the characters' lives.

This ability to leap from the trivial to the enduring, from frivolous details to painful truths, is Yates's specialty. He etches one ordinary phrase or common usage on the reader's mind, usually in such a way as to connect it with a large emotion or universal idea. Many writers over-whelm the reader with such effects, but Yates seems to move rapidly though a description and halt only for the right detail. Take for example the portrait of Walter Grimes, the girls' hard-working, long-suffering father. After the parents divorce, Walter brings his daughters for a visit to his office at the *New York Sun*. Sarah asserts that the *Sun* is the best paper; when her father corrects her, she asks why he works there. "Oh, I suppose if I were very talented I might move on, but I'm just—you know—I'm only a copy-desk man" (*EP,* 7). The "copy-desk man" comes up again where the sisters are drinking at Sarah's after their mother's devastating stroke. Superficially, they discuss their memories, recalling places and episodes in their parents's lives, but more profoundly they are troubled by their father's failure. Why did he never remarry and start over? Sarah comments that she didn't think "he ever understood why he was only—you know—only a copy-desk man" (*EP,* 136).

Pookie's tragic limitations are rendered through similar images and swift scenes. Her confused life is brought into focus by two descriptions. The first comes early: "She pored over fashion magazines, dressed taste-fully and tried many ways of fixing her hair but her eyes remained bewildered, and she never quite learned how to keep her lipstick within the borders of her mouth, which gave her an air of dazed and vulnerable uncertainty" (*EP,* 7). The dazed and bewildered aspects of her personal-ity are all there is after her stroke. Again at this point, the lipstick reap-pears as a motif: the poor woman "studied her frowning reflection and daubed a full crimson mouth on the surface of the mirror" (*EP,* 141). Here she describes a visit from JFK, who she fantasizes is her son-in-law: "After his press conference . . . he called me Pookie and gave me a little kiss. Such a handsome figure of a man, with that beautiful smile. He has such—such flair. Just imagine! The youngest man ever elected President in American history" (*EP,* 140).

Yates has picked up "flair" and worried that fashion magazine cliché into a new meaning. Working with a small but carefully selected group of such words and images, he produces his poignant effects: Tony and Sarah's picture in the rotogravure, their entwined-arms toasting ritual, Pookie's pretentious naming of their country place, Walter Grimes's calling his daughter "little rabbit" (*EP,* 33). The economical use of these devices keeps the narrative from having the drawn-out, dull quality one finds in long stretches of *A Special Providence.* Emily's identifying locution is "I see"—usually following some devastating information. This rather intellectual girl and woman reacts to embarrassment (about sex), shock (about Pookie), and disappointment (over Dunninger) with those two colorless, Hemingwayesque syllables.

Through skillful underuse, Yates avoids the pitfall of creating what E. M. Forster termed "flat" characters. Yates's reader never quite expects Emily's "I see" in the same way that Dickens's reader can predict the recurrence of "I will never desert Mr. Micawber." Because it lacks grandeur, even Yates's omnipresent false prediction "We'll be all right" usually passes unnoticed on first reading. At one key point in *The Easter Parade* he even switches "I see" from Emily's mouth to Sarah's and still leaves the discerning reader aware of its odd appropriateness coming from Sarah here: Emily must withdraw from her battered sister her prior invitation to move in because "I'm not living alone now." Sarah responds, "Oh. You mean you have a—I see" (*EP,* 169). At such a moment Yates lets Sarah share her sister's lifelong phrase, one she has always hated, while using it to express her shame, chagrin, and repression. (Tolstoy does the same thing with the lawyerly locutions of Ivan Illych, which are turned against him by his own doctor.)

The book's cumulative effect is also achieved by other devices: use of negative references to business and culture, and disturbingly rapid transitions that make years melt away in a paragraph. The latter technique makes *The Easter Parade* seem like a big book, when in fact it can easily be read in two short sittings. Yates moves us through the late depression by moving the Grimes sisters from Tenafly to Larchmont to "another town after Bradley, and then still another; in the last town, Sarah graduated from high school" (*EP,* 17). Using the locales of New York and its suburbs as markers of time, Yates parades Emily and us through Green-

if not his most successful, novel about the middle classes at midcentury. Where *The Easter Parade* moves with terrifying swiftness, this book unfolds slowly. And where *The Easter Parade* privileges its women and puts down the men, *Young Hearts Crying* exposes Lucy and Michael Davenport to equivalent amounts of harsh judgment, embarrassment, and disappointment.

Young Hearts Crying is a sustained presentation of two Americans' misfires: saying the wrong thing, promising what you can't deliver, expecting the unreasonable, pursuing careers that never jell. Unlike books where the miseries of faulty performing are spread around, *Young Hearts Crying* divides them evenly between two misguided people. Dialogue in the mouths of Yates's fleetingly minor characters can ring false—as when he quotes in passing some hippie types who sound more like Dead End kids, or when he makes an upper-class stockbroker inarticulately describe his admiration for a "no-bullshit" painter—but his portraiture of his main characters is always dead center. Each section carefully charts some loss of face for Michael or Lucy. The occasional complement to Yates's yearning couple—Ann Blake, the latest pathetic version of the mother as loser, or Carl Traynor, an edgier, prose-writing version of Jack Flanders—act as foils or supply an audience for dramatic outbursts. Generally, however, the minor characters in *Young Hearts Crying* are happier than Michael and Lucy.

Although the plot and the language are not especially complex, they work because of Yates's technique of juxtaposing and revisiting earlier scenes rather than merely repeating them. Yates all but acknowledges his tendency to double back on his successful phrases and observations, as when he has Michael self-consciously realizing that he had only "said six or eight funny things in his life, and that what passed for his sense of humor would always depend on a skillful recycling of old material, over and over again" (*YHC,* 227). Phrasings and whole scenes in *Young Hearts Crying* have their analogues decades and hundreds of pages apart: years after an alcoholic's stomach is turned by the sight of a huge raisin cookie, her alcoholic husband is equally sickened by a raisin cookie that "looked like a meal in itself"; punches are traded not once, but twice; a woman who compares her husband's craftmanship invidiously to Tennessee Williams's later performs clumsily in one of his plays (*YHC,* 211, 311). Yates coaxes larger meanings out of each of these reiterations.

The structure of this book, too, recapitulates that of Yates's first novel. In both novels, a well-favored, highly educated couple sets out to make a life after World War II. Michael, a new version of Frank

Wheeler, is mature about earning his living, in this incarnation refusing
to live off his immensely rich wife. Unlike Frank, he has some raw talent
as a poet, but instead of meeting deadheads in western Connecticut, he
is challenged by the talented bohemian Paul Maitland, his golden sister,
Diana, and later Tom Nelson, a painter of the first order.

These suburbs
are a bohemian nightmare rather than the bourgeois nightmare of *Revolutionary Road;* Lucy and Michael, after a brief period living a few Greenwich Village blocks from where the Wheelers lived, are transplanted to
Larchmont and later to Putnam County, where arty people are not in
short supply.

Part 1 opens in 1947 with 23-year-old war veteran Michael imagin-
ing himself as a cool skeptical poet. By the end of this part, he has
become the person doubted rather than the doubter, the hopelessly
awkward striver whose work is rejected. By age 35, he hears his no-
longer-adoring wife's appraisal: "And I'll tell you something else. A poet
is someone like Dylan Thomas. And a playwright—Oh, God—is someone like Tennessee Williams" (*YHC*, 96). Lucy is an upper-class version
of April Wheeler; prep school at "Farmington" and Radcliffe haven't
focused her, and she is trying to be an actress and trying to find people
to admire. At first, it's Michael ("You just—know so much"); soon it's
Paul and Diana Maitland (*YHC*, 5). The admiration is comparable to
April's sterile dream of golden friends, recontextualized in another book
about yearning.

In *Young Hearts Crying* this couple actually meets such people only to
find a source of embarrassment. Tom Nelson is a painter who uses old
pieces of wood and scratchy brushwork to fashion pictures that the
Museum of Modern Art wants: he achieves his effects with hardly any
effort and is as cool and casual as Michael is worrisome, clumsy, and self-
conscious. Michael struggles to impress Nelson with his book of poems
and has his work pronounced "nice." He fusses with his image (recall
Frank Wheeler) and wants to refer to his Golden Gloves defeat on the
dust jacket of his first book. In curiously neurotic but very Yatesian
manner, he wants to "work a light, self-deprecating touch into something like this." Lucy's response, foreshadowing their divorce, is
adamant: "I don't like it" (*YHC*, 45). Part 1 is largely about people who
misunderstand Michael.

Part 2 concentrates on Lucy's story: from the early 1950s well into
the late 1960s, Lucy moves from acting to writing to painting. The acting "career" is accompanied by a romance with sexy Jack Halloran,
a director at a little theater in Putnam County. Yates has used his old

theater troupe from *Revolutionary Road* (having someone overdo the performance) and made Lucy into something of a spectacle. This rich girl overdoes the role of Tennessee Williams's Blanche Dubois: the part of Blanche compounds the irony of a bored Radcliffe girl looking for thrills in a small-time playhouse. Jack, a commanding presence among a motley crew of amateurs, winds up being as brutal as Stanley Kowalski himself. (Yates's friend Kurt Vonnegut used the same backdrop, a couple playing Stanley and Blanche in an amateur production of *A Streetcar Named Desire* who fall in love, in his story "Who Are We This Time?"— a far more lighthearted version, needless to say, than Yates's.) Jack essentially tells Lucy that she's stagy and ordinary. After using her sexually, he goes on to a new job.

Lucy then drifts into the creative writing scene at the New School in Greenwich Village, where she meets a teacher and a student who criticize her short stories. Carl Traynor, a novelist who teaches poorly, is used by Yates as his latest image of himself. Again, he is self-lacerating and ultimately, like Flanders and Michael Davenport, wearisome to the woman who once admired him. The disease of literary failure—flat writing, predictable story lines, hokey sentiment—is, however, most obvious in Lucy herself. Her story "Summer Stock" is taken apart by a shrewd student named George Kelly, an elevator repairman who nonetheless knows a pat "comes-to-realize" story when he sees it. Lucy tries to revise her work but winds up turning to painting instead. She directs some of Kelly's criticisms at Carl Traynor's second novel and eventually erodes her confidence in him altogether.

This cat's cradle of weakness and judgment, pathetic striving and painful reckoning, soon includes two painters who look at Lucy's Art Students League work. Paul Maitland says she's learned a lot. Tom Nelson politely declares her an amateur. This part of the novel has also filtered Michael's story through Lucy's distracted, unsettled consciousness. While she's having her troubled affair with Halloran and her career setbacks, she learns that Michael is cracking up in New York City. And just as she imagines Halloran cheating on her with another actress and humiliating her, she imagines Michael in Bellevue being humiliated.

Part 3 returns to Michael's story, a similar version of romantic and professional disillusionment. After he and Lucy separate, his life falls into two periods: pre-Bellevue and post-Bellevue. Before his crack-up, he has two major affairs, both of them highlighting his age and vulnerability. An English twit named Jane Pringle throws him over, and then a young Vassar grad, engaged to one of Michael's friends, has a premarital fling with him—or would have, if not for his impotence. He nearly tests

himself a third time, but his friend Tom Nelson ruins it. He and Tom go
to Montreal for a TV production of a one-act play Michael has written;
an inviting girl is on the scene, but Tom won't let Michael make his
move on her, and indeed seems to take sadistic pleasure in frustrating
Michael's sexual urge.

After Bellevue, Michael has a second breakdown at a writer's conference in New Hampshire in 1964. Moving through well-used material,
Yates makes Michael a real writer, unlike the quasi-literary John Wilder,
who cracks up at a Vermont college in *Disturbing the Peace*. Pulling himself together after a stay at a psychiatric facility, Michael finds comfort
with Sarah Garvey, his daughter Laura's guidance counselor. They marry
and move to the midwest, but once again, the old Yates pattern starts to
form: an insightful woman gets wise to a weak man. This final section is
also a brilliantly orchestrated collection of other letdowns, patterns of
defeat that Michael is embarrassed to acknowledge.

Whether it involves Sarah or old friends, this last portion of the novel
brings on the awkwardness and humiliation of a lifetime. Michael either
repeats previous mistakes or revisits places where he went wrong.
Sophoclean without being tragic, this outcome is about a man who must
face the chilling wrongness of his own decisions in the past. Yates manages to pile up the ironies in order to express a large sense of Michael's
diminished life.

In an earlier section Michael has traded punches with a party guest;
here he trades punches with Paul Maitland (brother of glamorous
Diana), a patronizing friend who for years misunderstands Michael's
work for *Chain Store Age*—he had thought Michael worked for *Chain
Saw Age*. Michael must explain to him at this late date that he wrote
about stores that operate "in—you know—in chains," chains that
metaphorically describe the shackling effect such writing had on him as
well (*YHC*, 269). Later Michael will be in turn be knocked down psychologically in an awkward scene; he'll find that Paul is still the smug,
cool evaluator who can calmly pronounce while Michael sweats. Maitland warmly defends one of Michael's antithetical figures, the super-
successful Tom Nelson. And as Michael attempts to explain that Nelson
"can be a prick when he puts his mind to it," he talks too much and
makes himself a fool—both for Maitland and for his young wife, Sarah
(*YHC*, 313).

Mortifying incidents multiply; they tumble out of each episode. In
Billings, Kansas, as a writing teacher struggling with a traditional literary career amid a trendy 1960s faculty, Michael makes his ideas for
poems and his opinions of people into so many small defeats. When he

explains to young Sarah, now the mother of his newborn daughter, that he wants to write about Bellevue, vulnerability, and impotence, the dumbstruck girl turns on him, replicating Lucy's defining moment of rejection. She has been cool to the latest volume of understated poems ready for the publisher.

He is also ill at ease with his colleagues. An acquaintance from his Greenwich Village days, a waiter at the Blue Mill Tavern, has stopped to renew old ties before joining an infantry unit in Vietnam. Michael uses the young man's fate to set off bad feelings: he asks a party of liberal arts professors to give the boy a hand of applause. After a few hand claps, a professor's wife attacks the kid as a killer of women and children, putting Michael in a ticklish moral spot. A bland relativist would mediate the gaffe smoothly, and a macho absolutist would create a scene at the risk of losing his comfortable job. Although a macho type out to prove himself, Michael nevertheless seems wimpy and belligerent at the same time, a man of strong feelings who backs down. (Yates isolated this chapter of *Young Hearts Crying* and published it as a separate story with the Henry James–like title—and with Jamesian delicate morality—"The Right Thing.") For Michael and for Yates, the key question is whether there is a right way to do things, or if there is an ever-changing array of perfectly acceptable moral positions. Altogether, what comes to light in this section is the futility of trying to love, be popular, and write well.

At the end of the book, Sarah's affections are in doubt, and old friends have been discredited. It is time for Michael to take stock of his life and his art. He meets Lucy in Cambridge, in a scene echoing the disillusionment at the end of Flaubert's *A Sentimental Education:* two old friends reminisce about old times and might-have-beens. When Michael and Lucy return to the scene of their youthful love, they rehash their old conversations about writing and painting. "Fuck Art," she concludes after expressing her own frustration. Of course Michael can't agree, poet that he is; but as Lucy put it, the sentiment might cause him to "relax for the first time in your life" (*YHC,* 345). The book ends not with a "comes-to-realize" scene but with a slight yet definite lifting of mood. Michael walks off after an evening with truth-telling Lucy, agreeing to shrug off sentiment and big expectations.

In dramatizing the embarrassments of the Davenports, Yates studies the American class system with a jeweler's eye. This late volume allows itself time to identify the insults and injuries that Americans inflict on one another. Yates's bedeviled couple—a rich girl who can't succeed with talented middle-class people, a middle-class young man who can't handle the tension of being half office worker, half artist—play out a script that forces them to inflict pain and endure it. Lucy's money is a dark force lurking behind their actions; while they have agreed not to live off it, they haven't calculated the falseness of being an average couple in Greenwich Village with an extraordinary dormant fortune. Uneasy about what is hardly spoken of, they push forward without the weapons of available big money or pronounced talent.

Michael, overcompensating for having a rich wife who could keep him, becomes a familiar kind of social menace: the person who pushes to prove his worth. He hurts people and damages his relationships even as he tries to be smart and civil and virtuous. Depicted by a nineteenth-century English novelist, Michael would have been the bounder, insinuating his way into the lives of better endowed, better born, and more successful people. Yates portrays him as a bigmouth who violates the proprieties not because he's a superior person but because he has driven himself to be special. In trying so hard, he mistakes all the rules of society: he manages to arouse the mocking nature of Tom Nelson, to sneer at a once-famous homosexual actor, and to punch out complacent party guests. His transgressions all involve a failure to calculate the niceties of modern upper-bohemian society: he brings an awkward, intense, 1940s conception of himself—poet, boxer, tailgunner, skeptic—to bear on a cool postwar America of self-possessed artists and trendy beautiful girls.

Lucy is clumsy in her own upper-class ways. A dabbler who thinks that the arts are made for self-expression rather than the display of skill and vision, she writes short stories in a prose that, to her embarrassment, expresses her class position and her delicate sensitive nature. They are the ho-hum outpourings of a preppie who wants to be as special as her more talented husband. Her upper-class provinciality also surfaces as she tries to get in with the right people in the Village. Yates all but repeats April's line about golden people, this time making them top-notch artists. Lucy also displays her insecurity, snobbery, and meanness as she patronizes Michael—he's not, after all, Tennessee Williams. In the end, after she has given up the artistic illusion (and, in a second attempt to be someone else, given all her money to Amnesty International), she is something of a shell, an April Wheeler who doesn't kill herself.

Long Island in Time of War

Cold Spring Harbor, Yates's last completed book, lacks the duration and magnitude of *Young Hearts Crying* and *The Easter Parade;* instead it surveys the late 1930s and war years in the more contracted manner of *A Special Providence,* concentrating on parents and children rather than on siblings or couples. The return to the smaller scale boxes Yates in, forcing him to focus on a few characters: again the irresponsible, garrulous, genteel mother, appearing here under the name of Gloria Drake; her son, Phil, cut from the same bolt of cloth as Yates's other adolescents; Phil's divorced father, the benign, long-suffering office worker who buys his son the wrong suits for prep school. A new addition to this familiar acting company is Phil's sister, Rachel, a vulnerable, illusion-filled young girl, something like Sarah in *The Easter Parade*. This nuclear family resembles the one at the beginning of *The Easter Parade*, except that Yates has made the siblings' genders conform once again to his own. Like Yates's family, the mother, son, and daughter are living in genteel poverty in an unfashionable Greenwich Village apartment when one day, much like Sarah's fateful meeting of Tony in *The Easter Parade*, they meet another family whose fate entwines with theirs.

The Shepards, father and son, have their car break down on a visit to the city, and they happen to ring the Drakes' doorbell to call a garage. The father, Captain Shepard, is a weakling, a retired army man who clings to his title for dignity, living on Long Island with his neurasthenic, alcoholic wife. Their son, Evan, is a more likeable version of Tony Wilson in *The Easter Parade*, one with a limited vocabulary and oil-spattered T-shirt instead of an English accent and a cutaway. Yates gives some access to Evan's thought processes here—for long stretches he is the book's point-of-view character—and Evan is Yates's most convincing sketch of a character who bears few biographical similarities to Yates. Evan's frustrations, as he struggles to find a career and as he woos and then grows to detest his first wife, are pithily described.

The main narrative thread is the story of Evan Shepard and Rachel Drake. Yates uses their courtship and early days of marriage in Cold Spring as a framework to write on one of his favorite themes: small expectations. This couple has few of the ambitions—and none of the pretensions—of the Wheelers, the Davenports, or even the Groves and Prentices. Yates has returned instead to the lower-middle-class environment of *Eleven Kinds of Loneliness*, the faint hopes of people cut off from larger dreams. Evan has grown up with one passion: his love for cars. After divorcing Mary Donovan, a strong-headed young woman with some ambitions and plans for achieving them, Evan works on cars, living at home, helping support the young daughter he'd had with Mary.

He shares with Rachel the absence of ambition: she is content to marry Evan if only to break out of the frustrating relationship she has with her crazy mother; she regales her new husband with humiliating tales of Gloria's neuroses, to which Evan responds with pleasure. These two limited people, like the couples in *Eleven Kinds of Loneliness,* take pleasure in their limitations. *Eleven Kinds of Loneliness,* however, is strongly laced with irony, and each story shows its unhappy couples in a perspective that reveals their limitations clearly. *Cold Spring Harbor* is less ironic and occasionally asks the reader to sympathize with Evan and Rachel and take their narrow-focused vision seriously. The fragile Rachel shares some of Emily Grimes's infelicitous sensibility: Yates writes of the "quick erotic visions [coming] into Rachel's mind. They could get laid on the hearth rug by firelight."[4]

Cold Spring Harbor seems mired in the desperation of these half dozen stateside onlookers of World War II. Whereas *A Special Providence* alternates between the ravaged European theater of war and a shabby New York City, *Cold Spring Harbor* treats the era through Selective Service reject Evan, his World War I veteran father, and potential draft bait Phil. Playing no great role in their lives, the war principally serves as an occasion for Evan to brood over the inadequacies that earned him his 4-F status, or for Phil to daydream about military glory that would allow him to condescend to his big, capable brother-in-law, who treats him cavalierly. Yates's concern with the resentment these characters (and the others) feel toward one another is stronger than his attempt to evoke the period in any cohesive way. Regrettably, the confessing overwhelms the chronicling. The best episodes in *Cold Spring Harbor* merely add details to the Yates family cycle: parents divorcing, the broken family moving from house to house, the children suffering, the resentments emerging as the children struggle into adulthood and begin to separate from the deeply neurotic mother.

Even as Yates returns to the rag-and-bone shop of his unhappiness, he creates several effective scenes. Gloria Drake, like one of Charles Dickens's caricatures of his mother, is the subject of the most believable scenes. Her relentless absurdity and dopey gentility unify this choppy and sometimes labored book. Yates is at his best describing her endless talk on the day she first meets Evan and Captain Shepard. The "crappy little place" (Evan's assessment of the West Village apartment) and the time-filling nonsense that Gloria utters are perfectly coordinated. The smell of "cat droppings and cosmetics and recent cooking" affront Evan and Captain Shepard at the Drakes' door. Gloria first appears to Captain Shepard as "a nice person down on her luck. New York was honeycombed with this kind of wretched gentility" (*CSH,* 20).

In a matter of a half dozen pages, Yates produces fine sketches of woe. Like Pookie's presentation in *The Easter Parade,* Gloria's girlish manner and laugh called attention "to how loose and ill-defined her lips were" (recall Pookie's lipstick; *CSH,* 21). Yates writes about "the long runs of [her voice], the little bursts and hesitations of it, and the incipient hysteria" (*CSH,* 22). She "was ready to give her heart away to total strangers on the street"; she could talk "until veins the size of earthworms stood out in her temples." (*CSH,* 22). Her lack of self-control is inherited by Rachel, who winds up gushing to Evan (after some hours of acquaintanceship), "I think you're wonderful" (*CSH,* 26).

The themes of Gloria's household are bewilderment and lack of control. The vast bewilderment of her life, and her children's lives, can be warded off only by the sound of her own blather or a favorable glimmer in the mirror. Yates, of course, has dealt with this pattern before, not only in the versions of the weak mother (the overwrought performing narcissists) but also in numbers of his male characters who can't quite control their mouths or contain their self-absorption. As we listen to Gloria's genial palaver, we hear a dying echo of Frank Wheeler, another talker caught up in his own words. Gloria loves to contemplate herself in the mirror, thinking of herself as "congenial" (recall Frank Wheeler taking stock of his image in *Revolutionary Road* and Bobby Prentice posing in *A Special Providence*). In the end it is Gloria who completes Yates's procession of garrulous losers. "I didn't talk too much, did I?" she asks her son (*CSH,* 29).

Another finely rendered scene of diminishment involves Gloria's meeting with Captain Shepard. Now the setting is a midtown bar: the loss is not just a vague sense of foolishness but a definite tactical defeat. Captain Shepard wants Gloria to help take the pressure off Evan to marry Rachel. Although Gloria had intended to press hard for a wedding, Shepard is buying the drinks and soon has her tripping over her own feebly held principles, eating her own words, and thinking, "Maybe you have to have a man's mind to think as straight and as clearly as that" (*CSH,* 42). Like many of her predecessors in the Yates canon, she has been manipulated and forced to pretend that everything is all right.

Throughout the book, Gloria herself has manipulated people, only to see her plans collapse. She has convinced Rachel and Evan to rent a house with her in Cold Spring Harbor, yet it's only a matter of time before she grates on them and is cast off. In preparation for the devastating event, Yates devises one of his best family blowouts. (Recall that *Revolutionary Road* began with a spectacular quarrel between Frank and April Wheeler, a savage battle caused by April's disappointment and Frank's smugness.) The dynamics of this final disaster are similar to those in *Revolutionary Road:* a woman's image of herself is dashed by an indifferent world. As the scene opens, tormented Gloria anxiously measures her worth at a time when her daughter, a new mother, is still in the hospital and inevitably the center of attention. For the second time, Gloria goes with Captain Shepard on family business; they take a cab to the hospital, and all the while Gloria thinks of little jokes about not feeling "like a grandmother." This time, the disaster is more than a matter of being out-talked. Her daughter, Rachel, doesn't think of her mother as anyone but a destructive interloper. Gloria, psyched up for a good performance (and a drink afterward with Captain Shepard), instead runs head-on into Rachel's harsh digs about Gloria's child rearing. Like April eight books ago, Gloria goes wild with chagrin and embarrassment when faced with the truth. And like April she lashes out at her spouse, the bland, ineffectual Curtis Drake. On hand to see the new baby, Curtis receives his ex-wife's abuse. He's the cause of the children's poor upbringing; he's the coward. Gloria is soon hustled out of the room, and in effect from this point on, she is branded a crazy woman and banished from Rachel's affections.

The scenes after Rachel returns with the new baby are desolate: poor Gloria, filled with shame and unable to face the cruel tormentors, has kept to her room for weeks. Almost like some dotty suburban Gregor Samsa, she lives apart from the family that cares nothing for her. The pathos of this last tale of mother and child constitutes a kind of atonement for the sadism of *A Special Providence;* Gloria's fate stands out against the vague background of her children's struggles.

The other minor characters enjoy their small triumphs. Phil slowly overcomes his reputation as a do-nothing and a sissy. He takes a job as a parking attendant at a North Shore restaurant, makes some good money over the summer, and is able to buy a bike and a tweed jacket. But these triumphs are weakened by the strong undercurrent of social class that runs through the book. Self-determination is always spoiled by snobs, one's parents, and one's own anxiety. The bike has troubled Phil since a local rich boy, Flash Ferris, advanced him the money. To be beholden to no one—and especially not to Flash, the most egregious turkey at prep school—is Phil's goal. Predictably, for a character in Yates's own boyhood situation, Phil takes a cool view of country estates, servants, and fine living, although he is "polite in the best private-school manner" (*CSH*, 145–46). The North Shore gentry are buffoons and fossils, just the kind of people Gloria Drake would like Phil to cultivate. Flash, for his part, would like to buy, and thereby control, a friend. But Phil has other ideas: he would like to work, keep a polite distance from Flash, and wash his hands of the taint of snobbery and sycophancy. He pays off his debts and then readies himself for the fall term.

But here again Yates mounts an attack on the best-laid plans of an ambitious boy. Just when the time comes to get the holy tweed jacket, Curtis takes Phil to a midtown retail outlet and buys him two doubtful suits instead. The store scene—complete with wise-guy salesman and anxious consumer—is pure Yates; everything generates unease: "The two suits, brown and blue, had begun to worry Phil a little because he suspected they might be all wrong for the Irving School; even so, they had the look of valuable merchandise in the salesman's quick hands as he folded them in a tricky way and nestled them one after the other into separate suitcase-sized cardboard boxes that were then lashed together with clear yellow twine" (*CSH*, 175). Yates can't help returning to the scene of transgression that he first conjured up in *A Good School;* this time those wrong suits are treated with wry humor rather than distress.

But a notable triumph over middle-class misery is to be found in the story of a young Jewish boy who works with Phil in the roadside café. Aaron's co-workers throw him a party on his last night before joining the army. Here Yates has one of his last chances to deal with his genera-tion and the impact of the war. Aaron is a spokesman for the Yatesian point of view: he's no football hero and basically he's too wise (even in his teens) to believe what the movies say about war—or love, for that matter. The only thing he knows is that the truth for him might be fighting for his people as an infantryman or languishing as a payroll clerk in Nebraska. But whether the future contains glory or mere drudgery, the present is charged with the peculiar understated Yates pathos. We've heard the story of baffled kids at the brink of war in *A Good School:* here it is again, controlled yet deeply expressive. Phil, for one, would "sleep like a fool after the party" (*CSH,* 137).

And *Cold Spring Harbor* settles the reader down by compassionately dealing with Gloria, sending Phil back to school, giving Rachel and Evan a new start with their young child, and hustling off Captain Shep-ard and his wife. The bravura set pieces and domestic explosions in *Rev-olutionary Road* and *Disturbing the Peace* have been muted, making *Cold Spring Harbor* closest, in its quiet, matter-of-fact tones, to *A Good School,* but without the need to tie up each character's fate in slambang dra-matic fashion.

Chapter 7

Eleven Books of Loneliness: Unfinished and Minor Works

Richard Yates spent his career trying to recreate the magic of his first novel, and in his view, he never quite matched that early performance.[1] In the nine books described thus far, he dealt resolutely with the types of characters that *Revolutionary Road* laid bare, and he continued to write a remarkably consistent prose. The spare, precise prose style of *Cold Spring Harbor* is indistinguishable from that of *Revolutionary Road;* finding stylistic differences between "early Yates" and "late Yates" requires an angstrom microscope.[2] Yates scoffed at the idea he might try writing in a genre other than fiction: "I wouldn't know how to write a poem. Like most writers, I've messed around with it a little, just enough to find out how difficult it is . . . [although] you can fake a poem a lot more easily than you can fake a story. And as for plays, I tried to turn one of my stories into a one-act play once, many years ago, and I couldn't even finish it. I couldn't even get it down. It requires a different kind of nerves and muscles than I have" (Ross, 536). (The story he tried adapting was "The Best of Everything" [Henry, 68].) Nevertheless, certain fragments outside of the nine published works of fiction argue that his talent was more various, and more capable of growth, than that body of work might suggest.

Some of these fragments are available: Yates published bits of verse at one point in *Esquire* magazine, for example. He was inspired to compose some haiku-like compositions on the typewriter, limiting himself to the second row of the keyboard. The title and first half of a poem show his firm grip on such techniques as meter and caesura:

A Confession of Fulbrights
We were poor, we were witty
Our poetry tip-top, our Europe pretty.[3]

The other genre he worked in, screenwriting, earned him a handsome salary at several points in his career. Although never filmed, Yates's screenplay of William Styron's novel *Lie Down in Darkness* was published in 1988 by Ploughshares Press, constituting Yates's tenth published book.

Yates admired Styron's work enormously, and it is not hard to see why. Both men wrote work after work about troubled middle-class characters, in a realistic vein. Their books were always serious studies that critics routinely found bleak. The difference was that Styron made a living selling such fiction, and from that living occupied an upper-middle-class place in society always denied to Yates. Styron's success inspired Yates to keep plugging away at his craft. *Lie Down in Darkness*, a novel whose heroine never resolves a troubled relationship with her father, was a more sensational, Southern version of a Yatesian family tragedy. (It differed in its neo-Gothic, somewhat melodramatic, and always heightened sense of gloom, concluding with the heroine's suicide in the book's final pages. The deaths of characters in Yates's fiction are surprisingly few for a writer accused of morbidness—April Wheeler, John Quint, Sarah Grimes—and only April's death after a self-inflicted abortion even resembles suicide.) George Bluestone, in his introduction to the screenplay, points out several useful touches Yates applied to Styron's novel that made the screenplay sing. (Yates was offered scriptwriting jobs as often as he was, no doubt, because of his routinely brilliant dialogue, particularly heated exchanges between family members.)

The Bridge at Remagen was Yates's "successful" attempt at writing screenplays—successful only in the sense that the screenplay was filmed and released (in 1969, starring George Segal). Yates was always dissatisfied with the screenplay, which, like *A Special Providence,* tells the story of an American army platoon on maneuvers in northern Europe in the final months of World War II. Unlike *A Special Providence,* however, Yates had to collaborate with two other writers and had to labor under the war-movie genre's demand for constant action. The army chapters in *A Special Providence* are the weakest in a weak novel, and the descriptions of warfare are the weakest spots within those chapters. *The Bridge at Remagen* will remain as Yates's sole legacy to Hollywood, until *Lie Down in Darkness* or other projects are filmed. (Woody Allen was interested in filming *The Easter Parade,* and Joe Pesci contracted to play John Wilder in *Disturbing the Peace.*)

Yates's unfinished novel *Uncertain Times* begins as William Grove, the writer-protagonist of *A Good School* and numerous short stories, has just returned from adapting a novel for Hollywood. It is New Year's Day 1963, and Grove's story picks up just about where Jack Field's story,

"Saying Goodbye to Sally," leaves off. *Uncertain Times* recounts the events of the most anomalous and in many ways exciting year of Yates's life, the eight months he worked for U.S. Attorney General Robert F. Kennedy, writing "everything that came out of his mouth" (Venant).

As Grove's presence indicates, Yates is again weaving a tale that is more than semiautobiographical. The events Yates describes—working closely with Bobby Kennedy during the tumultuous spring and summer of 1963—are action-packed and complicated. Why did Yates wait so long to write about these events? Possibly because he had been offered the job on the condition that he never describe in print the private discussions he heard and participated in within the administration. But since this explanation doesn't account for the many memoirs freely written after both Kennedys had died, it is likelier that Yates held back because of his ambivalence to the Kennedy brothers and their policies.

Throughout *Uncertain Times* Bill Grove describes himself as deeply suspicious of the Kennedys' policies, ambitions, and legend. He nearly disqualifies himself as a candidate for the speechwriting job when he openly confesses his negative attitude. For a brief spell, he gets religion and buckles down to write stirring speeches for both Kennedy brothers, but then relapses into mistrust and skepticism.

Unlike the family chronicles and the confessional musings of his last few books, *Uncertain Times* uses a tighter plot than Yates usually employed. Here alcoholism, blocked writing, and failed relationships present themselves once again, but now Yates can juxtapose these familiar elements of a stalled life against lives with a mission, frenetically go-go-going. The Kennedy administration whips like a tornado around the bewildered speechwriter, who slowly learns how to carry himself in that hypercharged air. The comparison, oddly, between Yates's own laboriously thoughtful approach and the Kennedy brothers' need to move at all costs favors neither the one nor the other. Yates has written the least idolatrous account of any Kennedy insider, showing all the foibles and neuroses of incessant action even as he depicts the excitement of the times and of that place. But instead of simply ridiculing his own torpid pace, as he generally did in his self-hectoring passages, here he has the Kennedys to pin the tail on, too. He shows how the work he did for them left him feeling used and lightly regarded. A sheet of alternate titles he was considering, aside from *Uncertain Times,* shows his disillusionment: one is *A Fool's Errand,* another *A Fool For Hire,* and so on—nine titles in all, every one but *Uncertain Times* labeling Yates a fool for taking the job in the first place.

Yates intended to counterpoint his political narrative—including
Grove's career at the Justice Department, the routine of speechwriting,
and the vicissitudes of public service—with a series of personal revela-
tions, some of them recycled from earlier works. One handwritten page
of Yates's notes counterpoints national events in the spring and summer
of 1963 with events in Grove's romantic life.

At the book's outset, he is living with a woman in a basement apartment in Greenwich Village. When the thinly disguised *Lie Down in
Darkness* production gets red-lighted, early that year, he half-heartedly
looks for work in his old field, PR writing, but strikes out. The scenes of
this job hunt are evocatively humiliating. But then Grove's luck
changes: Paul Cameron (in real life, William Styron) recommends him
for a job as RFK's wordmeister, and he's soon shuttling between Washington, D.C., and Greenwich Village, pounding out copy for "Bob" and
scrapping with his girlfriend about his integrity as a novelist versus the
hackwork of speechwriting.

Early on during the interview process, Yates introduces an element of
tension that never gets resolved in this unfinished manuscript: On his
job application, Grove has omitted his past nervous breakdowns, hospi-
talizations, and lingering alcoholism, and he is assured that the FBI
background check on him will be thorough and puritanical in its find-
ings. So through the entire experience of government work, Grove
knows that it's only a matter of time before he loses his well-paying job,
and he (and we) wait for the other shoe to fall.

The other tension in *Uncertain Times* cleverly concerns the parallel
conflicts in Grove's personal and professional lives. Bill's success at finding, auditioning for, and winning the speechwriting job is derided by his
Village girlfriend, who discourages him, reminds him of his own unfinished novel (plainly, by its plot, *A Special Providence*), and eventually
accompanies him to Washington, where she stages an "emergency" that
hauls him out of a meeting with the attorney-general. Representing his
old, sordid Village life, this girlfriend functions as Yates's women often
do, as a nagging reminder of the refined, artistic goals of a man too
weak to resist the temptations of creature comforts before him.
Whether she—or April Wheeler or the wife in "Regards at Home"—is
really looking out for her man's best interest, or simply jealous of his
success in his career, she belittles him to the point at which he desperately looks for a way out.

Plenty of pretty young women in 1963 Washington are willing to
take up with a Kennedy speechwriter, and Bill soon finds a new girl-

friend. He meets wholesome, healthy, and kind Holly Parsons, a secretary in the Justice Department, just when he's most enthusiastic about his job. For his audition, a Commencement Day speech for Kennedy to deliver at a Catholic girls' college, he had ingeniously laced the speech with subtle sexual undercurrents that won a powerful response from Kennedy's audience. Grove impresses Holly by continuing to write eloquent speeches for the most rhetorically attuned administration since Roosevelt's. But then he starts again to question the Kennedys' style, content, and integrity, rehashing a major theme in Yates: a character who achieves his goal and then questions harshly his motives for having had the goal. In *Uncertain Times* Yates has the Kennedys to stand for his baser impulses; in previous works, he was able to use only their photographs, as in *Disturbing the Peace,* and a minor figure such as Chester Pratt to represent a cynicism he mistrusted in himself. Here, the thematic tension is also plot-operative.

Another Yates theme, that of the self-conscious performing self, recurs here as well. Grove thinks of himself as an "in-house Abraham Lincoln" kept at the Justice Department "to write an in-house Gettysburg Address every once in a while." He also emphasizes the Kennedys' showmanship, the strained strategies, and the factitious side of being idealistic public servants. At one point he compares John Kennedy's looks to Amelia Earhart's. RFK is pictured trying to ingratiate himself with everybody, even the motorcycle cops accompanying his entourage. The overall impression of the exalted figures Grove works for is a highly ambivalent one, and that ambivalence is consistent with Grove's picture of himself.

At times, Grove seems to be showing the Kennedy brothers the right way to speak and generally to comport themselves; at other times, he seems a bumbling neophyte negotiating the sophisticated Washington world. Aware and eloquent though he is, Grove is too wised up and cynical for his own good. Yates's landscape of Washington is a place where great things may be happening, but where Bill Grove is a bit out of step with them. Yates also assigns him sexual potency problems with Holly (similar to the impotence scene in *Young Hearts Crying*), and the mix of political and personal weakness makes for a tense series of episodes, juxtaposed as it is with powerfully convincing scenes of authentic Washington life.

Yates's drawn-from-life characters and Washington scenes are consistently believable. Kennedy's associate "Blake Archer" is plainly the assistant attorney general for civil rights Burke Marshall; the former

Pulitzer Prize–winning reporter, press secretary "Jim Thurman," is Ed Guthman; the cigar-smoking, bow-tie-and-Brooks-Brothers-suit-wearing "Alfred Schindler" is Arthur Schlesinger; and so on.

The most authentic portions of *Uncertain Times* come when Yates goes into his astonishingly vast storehold of compelling detail about the art of speechwriting, and particularly when he goes into the mechanics of the trade. He reprints long passages of Grove's (and his) words that the Kennedys spoke as their own, analyzing the decisions behind his choice of these words. The sections on speechwriting in *Uncertain Times* stand as a strong argument for Yates as a versatile writer who deliberately chose to pursue a limited range of subject. Not only are the speeches themselves moving and effective, but it is obvious from reading *Uncertain Times* that they were crafted by a completely professional writer under difficult and tense circumstances. His friend E. Barrett Prettyman (who appears in this book under the name "Warren Pickering") commented on Yates's total integrity, and he worked alongside Yates at a time when that integrity was challenged daily.

Uncertain Times is Yates's unfinished masterpiece, not unlike F. Scott Fitzgerald's *The Last Tycoon,* a close study of a fascinating but largely unexplored period in the author's life, containing his freshest and most brilliant work in decades. Various conjectured endings have been added to published editions of Fitzgerald's final book, and *Uncertain Times* may yet be published as Yates's eleventh book of loneliness. The fine pacing, the off-center point of view, the consistently probing style, all make for a strong ending to a troubled career. Yates's voice—skeptical, self-effacing, and quietly judgmental—is one that needs to be heard more often. As it fills out a detailed, harsh account of American ambitions and disappointments from the 1930s to the 1970s, it can reconnect us with some of the best elements of the American realistic condition—clarity, craft, honesty.

Notes and References

Chapter One

1. Richard Yates, *Revolutionary Road* (Boston: Atlantic-Little, Brown, 1961); hereafter cited in text as *RR*.

2. See Michiko Kakutani's review of the Delta-Seymour Lawrence reprint of *RR, New York Times,* 25 April 1983; for good sociological material on the suburban landscape, see James Howard Kunstler's *The Geography of Nowhere* (New York: Simon and Schuster, 1994), hereafter cited in text.

3. For Yates's avowed influences, see his *New York Times Book Review* article "Some Very Good Masters"; also see "Authors Comment on Living Author They Most Admire," *New York Times Book Review,* 4 December 1977, 74, for Salinger's influence on Yates, and the 1972 *Ploughshares* interview.

4. Lionel Trilling, *The Liberal Imagination* (New York: Harcourt, Brace, Jovanovich, 1978), unpaginated preface.

5. C. Wright Mills, *White Collar: the American Middle Classes.* (New York: Oxford University Press, 1951); hereafter cited in text.

6. C. Frances Kiernan, "Group Encounter," *New Yorker,* 7 June 1993, 56–61.

7. Yates described his indebtedness to Fitzgerald in several places, particularly in his essay "Some Very Good Masters" and the story "Saying Goodbye to Sally" in *Liars in Love.*

8. Alexis De Tocqueville, *Democracy in America,* ed. J. P. Mayer, trans. George Lawrence (New York: Harper and Row, 1988), 2:627–32; hereafter cited in text.

9. Edmund Wilson, *A Piece of my Mind* (New York: Farrar, Straus, and Cudahy, 1956), 213; hereafter cited in text.

10. David Riesman, *The Lonely Crowd* (New Haven, Conn.: Yale University Press, 1974).

11. Richard Yates, *Eleven Kinds of Loneliness* (Boston: Atlantic-Little, Brown, 1962); hereafter cited in text as *11K.*

12. On Yates's middle-class consciousness, see David Castronovo, *The American Gentleman* (New York: Continuum, 1991), 79–80; also see below, chapter 2.

13. See Mills, *White Collar,* chapter 11.

14. For a discussion of distancing oneself from a job, see ibid., 257–58.

15. Erving Goffman, *The Presentation of Self in Everyday Life* (Garden City, N.Y.: Doubleday/Anchor Books, 1959), 17–76, 253; hereafter cited in text.

16. On the self and fashioning performances, see ibid., chapter 1. On the play-acting theme in Yates, see Jerome Klinkowitz, *The New American Novel of*

Manners: the Fiction of Richard Yates, Dan Wakefield and Thomas McGuane (Athens: University of Georgia Press, 1985), 20. Klinkowitz quotes Kurt Vonnegut's *Mother Night* to good effect: "We are what we pretend to be, so we must be careful what we pretend to be."

17. Richard Yates, *Young Hearts Crying* (New York: Delacorte, 1984), hereafter cited in text as *YHC*.

Chapter Two

1. *Richard Yates: An American Writer* (New York: Seymour Lawrence, 1993), 21, hereafter cited in text as *RY*.

2. DeWitt Henry and Geoffrey Clark, "An Interview with Richard Yates," *Ploughshares* 1 (December 1972): 70, hereafter cited in text.

3. F. Scott Fitzgerald, *Afternoon of an Author*, (New York: Scribner's, 1958), 132.

4. Peter Hastings Falk, ed., *Who Was Who in American Art*, compiled from the original thirty-four volumes of *American Art Annual: Who's Who in Art: Biographies of American Artists Active from 1898 to 1947* (Madison, Conn.: Sound View Press, 1985), 700–7011. Also see *Who's Who of American Women*, 2d ed. (Chicago: Marquis, 1962), 1091.

5. A brief account of this incident is in the *New York Times* of 16 April 1933, section 2, p. 3, col. 8.

6. Richard Yates, *A Special Providence* (New York: Knopf, 1969), hereafter cited in text as *ASP*. The phrase itself is a rare literary tag from Hamlet's speech, "There is special providence in the fall of a sparrow," which Yates embeds in Mrs. Prentice's consciousness with no overt reference to its source.

7. Elizabeth Venant, "A Fresh Twist in the Road: For Novelist Richard Yates, a Specialist in Grim Irony, Late Fame's a Wicked Return," *Los Angeles Times*, 9 July 1989, section 6, p. 1, col. 3; hereafter cited in text.

8. Sharon Yates Levine, interview with Steven Goldleaf, July 18, 1994, hereafter cited in text as SYL interview.

9. *Contemporary Authors*, vol. 10, ed. Deborah A. Straube, New Revision Series (Detroit: Gale, 1981), 535; hereafter cited in text as Ross.

10. Both Parker's and Beattie's blurbs were printed on the back cover of the Vintage reprint of *Eleven Kinds of Loneliness*.

11. David Streitfeld, "Book Report," *Washington Post*, December 27, 1992, p. X15, hereafter cited in text. The BU archive material also features correspondence to Yates when he was in the UCLA neuropsychiatric facility.

12. Richard Yates, *Disturbing the Peace* (New York: Delacorte, 1975), hereafter cited in text as *DTP*.

13. Letter in Boston University archives of Monica McCall, Richard Yates's literary agent from the early 1950s through the mid-1970s, hereafter cited in text as BU-MM.

14. Richard Yates, *The Easter Parade* (New York: Delacorte, 1976), 88, hereafter cited in text as *EP*.

15. Clark, 32–33.

16. Steven Goldleaf interview with Leslie Epstein, the director of the graduate program in creative writing at Boston University, 20 July 1994.

17. Monica Yates, interview with Steven Goldleaf, 16 October 1994; hereafter cited as MY interview. *The Independent,* 21 November 1992, article also mentions his Tuscaloosa living arrangements after his visiting appointment was over.

18. Scott Bradfield, "Follow the Long and Revolutionary Road," *The Independent,* 21 November 1992.

19. DeWitt Henry, telephone interview with authors, 25 July 1994; hereafter cited in text as DH interview.

20. *Stories for the Sixties,* ed. Richard Yates (New York: Bantam, 1963), vii.

Chapter Three

1. James Atlas, "A Sure Narrative Voice," *Atlantic Monthly* 248 (November 1981): 84.

2. In his discussion with Henry and Clark (p. 7), Yates acknowledged that his early drafts of *Revolutionary Road* were thick with the odor of soap operas, particularly the dialogue, and needed much revision to be cleansed of it.

3. Norman Mailer, in a three-part symposium, "Our Country and Our Culture," part 1 *Partisan Review,* May-June 1952, 299; hereafter cited in text as "Country."

4. Isaac Rosenfeld, *An Age of Enormity: Life and Writing in the Forties and Fifties* (Cleveland: World, 1962), 313.

5. Harold Rosenberg, "The Herd of Independent Minds," in *Discovering the Present: Three Decades In Art, Culture, and Politics* (Chicago: University of Chicago Press, 1973), 27–28, hereafter cited in text.

6. Reinhold Niebuhr, *The Irony of American History* (New York: Scribner's, 1952), chapter 8.

7. Orville Prescott, "Books of the Times," *New York Times,* 10 March 1961, p. 2, col. 3.

8. *Atlantic Monthly* 207 (April 1961): 115.

9. David Boroff, "Couple on Misery Row," *Saturday Review* 44 (25 March 1961): 21.

10. Theodore Solotaroff, "The Wages of 'Maturity,' " *Commentary,* July 1961, 8.

11. Jule Styne and Stephen Sondheim, "Some People," in *Gypsy: A Musical,* by Arthur Laurents (New York: Random House, 1959), 14.

Chapter Four

1. Quoted as a blurb on the Vintage Contemporaries edition of *Eleven Kinds of Loneliness.*

2. Quoted as a blurb of the Delta paperback edition of *Eleven Kinds of Loneliness.*

3. Quoted as a blurb in the prefatory matter to the Vintage Contemporary edition of *Eleven Kinds of Loneliness,* 1989.

4. Diana Trilling, *The Beginning of the Journey: The Marriage of Diana and Lionel Trilling* (New York: Harcourt, Brace, 1993), 341; hereafter cited in text.

5. A "comes-to-realize" story is Yates's term in *Young Hearts Crying* for a formulaic slick-magazine story with a heavy-handed epiphany.

6. J. D. Salinger also had an unpleasant woman surnamed "Snell" in "Down at the Dinghy" in *Nine Stories.*

7. Erving Goffman, *Stigma: Notes on the Management of Spoiled Identity* (Englewood Cliffs, N.J.: Prentice-Hall, 1963), 135.

8. Compare Yates's social ambiguities with the sharp satire employed by Terry Southern in another 1950s story with a similar setting and plot, "You're Too Hip, Baby" in *Red Dirt Marijuana.*

9. Peter Buitenhuis, *New York Times Book Review,* 25 March 1962, 4.

10. Richard Yates, *A Good School* (New York: Delacorte-Seymour Lawrence, 1978), 15; hereafter cited in text as *AGS.*

Chapter Five

1. On 16 March 1962 the producer Ingo Preminger wrote Yates's agent Monica McCall rejecting Yates's short stories, citing their depressing qualities, their plotlessness, and the characters' overwhelming tendency to alienate themselves from people, characteristics that make the stories eminently unsuitable for the television market (BU-MM).

2. J. D. Salinger, *Raise High the Roofbeams, Carpenters and Seymour an Introduction* (Boston: Little, Brown, 1963), 179.

3. "Builders" was the last story in *Eleven Kinds of Loneliness* to be written, and it was the only story written after the mid-1950s. It is in some significant ways anomalous—its style, its length, and its narrators are all out of keeping with the first collection and very much in keeping with the second.

4. Richard Rosen, "Heirs to Maxwell Perkins," *Horizon* 24 (April 1981): 50.

5. Letter from Yates's agent Mitch Douglas, dated 8 February 1979.

6. Richard Yates, *Liars in Love* (New York: Delacorte–Seymour Lawrence, 1981), 146–47; hereafter cited in text as *LIL.*

7. For all their collective years in Hollywood, both Fitzgerald and Yates wrote very few scripts that got produced and earned them screen credits; Fitzgerald got a credit on *Three Comrades* and Yates got one for *The Bridge at Remagen.* At various points, according to the BU archives, Yates was considered as the screenwriter for *Belle du Jour,* and may have worked on a screenplay for another World War II picture about Iwo Jima.

8. Sheilah Graham and Gerold Frank, *Beloved Infidel: The Education of a Woman* (New York: Holt, 1958). The date of *Beloved Infidel* and its popularity suggest that Fitzgerald's exploits in Hollywood with Graham were fresh in Yates's mind when he (and the fictional Jack Fields) flew out to Hollywood in March 1962.

9. F. Scott Fitzgerald, *The Crack-up,* ed. Edmund Wilson, (New York: New Directions, 1945), 212; hereafter cited in text.

10. Yates told Henry and Clark that he found "reprehensible" the trend toward personal journalism and straight autobiography usurping and contaminating fiction (Henry, 71). Clark finds Yates "astonishingly logical on literary matters of all kinds," though in the story "Liars in Love," Yates renders history out of sequence when he has the Rosenbergs being executed by the early spring of 1953, some three months too soon.

11. Brooks Landon, "Richard Yates," in *Yearbook 1981* (Detroit: Gale, 1981), 134.

Chapter Six

1. Richard Yates, *A Special Providence* (New York: Knopf, 1969), 29.

2. *Who's Who of American Women* lists Ruth Maurer Yates's address as "High Hedges" in St. James, N.Y., and Sharon Yates Levine confirmed that her grandmother had given that rather pretentious name to the rather unpretentious home of her in-laws.

3. Yates had often come under fire for writing in a way that was perceived as somehow hostile to women, rather than being highly judgmental of both sexes, dating as far back as the story "The B.A.R. Man," which Rust Hills, *Esquire's* fiction editor, had rejected on the ground that it was a woman-hating story. How Rust Hills could have so misread Yates's mockery of the title character's social limitations and made him out to be Yates's mouthpiece is nothing short of astonishing.

4. Richard Yates, *Cold Spring Harbor* (New York: Seymour Lawrence–Delacorte, 1986), 68; hereafter cited in text as *CSH.*

Chapter Seven

1. In the *Los Angeles Times* interview by Elizabeth Venant in 1989, Yates remarked, *"Revolutionary Road* remains my best book without question. I'm one of those writers who has the misfortune to write his best book first," repeating a sentiment he had voiced to Jean W. Ross in 1984: "I've been more than a little depressed at the thought of how much better *Revolutionary Road* is than the others all these years" (Ross, 536).

2. In 1984 Yates, asked about differences in his recent writing, noted changes in his pacing over the years: "I make fewer mistakes now, technically. Let me think for a moment. Well . . . I know when a new character can be introduced without a lot of background detail. And I know when a chapter can be hurried along. Generally I've acquired a better sense of pace" (Herbert Mitgang, "Moving the Story Along," *New York Times,* 28 October 1984, section 7, p. 3, col. 2).

3. Richard Yates, "QWERTYUIOP 1/2" *Esquire,* 66 (October 1966): 98.

Selected Bibliography

PRIMARY SOURCES

Cold Spring Harbor. New York: Seymour Lawrence–Delacorte, 1986.
Disturbing the Peace. New York: Seymour Lawrence–Delacorte, 1975.
The Easter Parade. New York: Seymour Lawrence–Delacorte, 1976.
Eleven Kinds of Loneliness. Boston: Atlantic–Little, Brown, 1962.
A Good School. New York: Seymour Lawrence–Delacorte, 1978.
Liars In Love. New York: Seymour Lawrence–Delacorte, 1981.
Revolutionary Road. Boston: Atlantic–Little, Brown, 1961.
A Special Providence. New York: Knopf, 1969.
William Styron's "Lie Down in Darkness": A Screenplay. Watertown, Mass.:
    Ploughshares, 1985.
Young Hearts Crying. New York: Seymour Lawrence–Delacorte, 1984.

BOOKS EDITED

Stories for the Sixties. New York: Bantam, 1963.

UNCOLLECTED FICTION AND ESSAYS

"Appreciation," *December*, vol. 23, nos. 1,2 (1981): 41–44.
"The End of the Great Depression," story, *Transatlantic Review* 11 (winter
    1962): 76–83.
"Lament for a Tenor," story, *Cosmopolitan*, vol. 136, February 1954, 50–57.
"R. V. Cassill's Clem Anderson," *Ploughshares*, 14, 2–3 (1988): 189–196.
"Some Very Good Masters," essay, *New York Times Book Review*, 19 April 1981, 3.
"Uncertain Times," selection from a novel, *Open City* 3 (1995): 35–71.

POETRY

"QWERTYUIOP 1/2," *Esquire*, vol. 66, October 1966, 98.

SECONDARY SOURCES

Atlas, James. "A Sure Narrative Voice" (review of *LIL*). *Atlantic Monthly* 248
    (November 1981): 84–85.
Baughman, Ronald. "Richard Yates." *Dictionary of Literary Biography Yearbook*,
    300–304. Detroit: Gale, 1992.
Boroff, David. "Couple on Misery Row" (review of *RR*). *Saturday Review* 44 (25
    March 1961): 21.
Bradfield, Scott. "Follow the Long and Revolutionary Road." *The Independent*,
    21 November 1992.

"Briefly Noted" (review of *RR*). *New Yorker* 37 (1 April 1961): 131.

Buitenhuis, Peter. "Windows Opened on Experience" (Review of *11K*). *New York Times Book Review,* 25 March 1962, 4.

Chappell, Fred. Essay on *Revolutionary Road.* In *Rediscoveries,* edited by David Madden, 245–55. New York: Crown, 1971.

Clark, Geoffrey. "The Best I Can Wish You." *Northeast Corridor,* vol. 1, no. 2 (1994): 26–41.

Cuomo, George. "Richard Yates: The Art of Craft." *Denver Quarterly* 19 (Spring 1985): 127–32.

Dubus, Andre. "A Salute to Mister Yates." *Black-Warrior-Review* vol. 15, no. 2 (Spring 1989): 160–161.

Edwards, Thomas R. "Only Yesterday" (review of *AGS*). *New York Review of Books,* 27 November 1978, 33.

Fishman, Ethan. "Natural Law and Right in Contemporary American Middle-Class Literature." In *Political Mythology and Popular Fiction,* ed. by Lee Sigelman. New York: Greenwood Press, 1988.

Henry, DeWitt. Review of *DTP. Ploughshares* 3.1 (1976): 159–65.

Kakutani, Michiko. Review of *RR. New York Times,* 25 April 1983.

Klinkowitz, Jerome. "Richard Yates: The Wedding of Language and Incident." In *The New American Novel of Manners: The Fiction of Richard Yates, Dan Wakefield, and Thomas McGuane,* 14–59. Athens: University of Georgia Press, 1986.

Larner, Jeremy. "An Enormous, Obscene Delusion" (review of *RR*). *New Republic* 144 (22 May 1961): 25.

Lehmann-Haupt, Christopher. Review of *AGS. New York Times,* 8 December 1978, 25.

Levin, Martin. "With a Fingerhold on Reality" (Review of *RR*). *New York Times Book Review,* 5 March 1961, 5.

Moynahan, Julian. Review of *AGS. New York Times Book Review,* 12 November 1978, 11.

Nelson, Ronald J. "Richard Yates's Portrait of the Artist as a Young Thug: 'Doctor Jack-o'-Lantern.' " *Studies in Short Fiction,* vol. 32, no. 1 (Winter 1995): 1–10.

Prescott, Orville. Review of *RR. New York Times,* 10 March 1961, 25.

Pritchard, William. Review of *DTP. Hudson Review,* vol. 29 (Spring 1976): 151–52.

Solotaroff, Theodore. "The Wages of 'Maturity' " (review of *RR*). *Commentary,* July 1961, 89.

Taylor, Anya. "A Thrice-Told Tale: Fiction and Alcoholism in Richard Yates's *Disturbing the Peace.*" *Dionysos: The Literature and Addiction TriQuarterly,* vol. 1, no. 3 (Winter 1990): 3–12.

Venant, Elizabeth. "A Fresh Twist in the Road: For Novelist Richard Yates, a Specialist in Grim Irony, Late Fame's a Wicked Return." *Los Angeles Times,* 9 July 1989, section 6, p. 1, col. 3.

WORKS OF CULTURAL AND SOCIAL CRITICISM

Castronovo, David. *The American Gentleman: Social Prestige and the Modern Literary Mind.* New York: Continuum, 1993.

Goffman, Erving. *The Presentation of Self in Everyday Life.* Garden City, N.Y.: Doubleday/Anchor Books, 1959.

———. *Stigma: Notes on the Management of Spoiled Identity.* Englewood Cliffs, N.J.: Prentice-Hall, 1963.

Kunstler, James Howard. *The Geography of Nowhere.* New York: Simon and Schuster, 1994.

Mills, C. Wright. *White Collar: The American Middle Classes.* New York: Oxford University Press, 1951.

Niebuhr, Reinhold. *The Irony of American History.* New York: Scribner's, 1952.

"Our Country and Our Culture." Three-part symposium in *Partisan Review* (May-June, July-August, September-October, 1952): 282–326, 420–450, 562–599.

Riesman, David. *The Lonely Crowd.* New Haven, Conn.: Yale University Press, 1948.

Rosenberg, Harold. *Discovering the Present: Three Decades in Art, Culture, and Politics.* Chicago: University of Chicago Press, 1973.

Rosenfeld, Isaac. *An Age of Enormity: Life and Writing in the Forties and Fifties.* Cleveland: World, 1962.

Tocqueville, Alexis de. *Democracy in America.* Edited by J. P. Mayer. Translated by George Lawrence. New York: Harper and Row, 1988.

Trilling, Diana. *The Beginning of the Journey: The Marriage of Diana and Lionel Trilling.* New York: Harcourt Brace Jovanovich, 1993.

Trilling, Lionel. *The Liberal Imagination.* New York: Harcourt Brace Jovanovich, 1978.

Wilson, Edmund. *A Piece of My Mind.* New York: Farrar, Straus and Cudahy, 1956.

Index

The Authors

David Castronovo is professor of English at Pace University and the author of four books: *Edmund Wilson, Thornton Wilder, The English Gentleman,* and *The American Gentleman.* He has edited and introduced *From the Uncollected Edmund Wilson* with Janet Groth, and contributed articles to *America, Commonweal,* and *Forward.*

Steven Goldleaf is associate professor of English at Pace University and the author of fiction, poetry, and essays appearing in a wide range of publications, among them *Partisan Review, The Colby Quarterly, Massachusetts Review, Kansas Quarterly,* and the *Bill James Baseball Abstract.*

The Editor

Frank Day is a professor of English and head of the English Department at Clemson University. He is the author of *Sir William Empson: An Annotated Bibliography* (1984) and *Arthur Koestler: A Guide to Research* (1985). He was a Fulbright lecturer in American literature in Romania (1980–81) and in Bangladesh (1986–87).